Astrology as a Therapeutic Art

Healing Human Relationships

I've long considered Greg Bogart to be perhaps the most insightful astrologer working today when it comes to illuminating the psychological dynamics of charts. In this wonderfully concise volume, a series of case studies display his seasoned understanding of those dynamics and clearly explain the psychotherapeutic context in which he approaches the birth chart. Astrologers of all orientations will derive useful insights from this work, but it is an especially invaluable asset for anyone considering entering into an actual career in counseling astrology.

—Ray Grasse, *The Waking Dream, Under a Sacred Sky,* and *An Infinity of Gods.*

Dr. Greg Bogart weaves astrology and mental health practice together, illustrating the counseling process with lucid case examples. I love his synopses of planetary psychodynamics and his overview of the history of humanistic–psychological astrology. Relatable, warm, and open, his command of his professions and care for his clients is clear. This book is another step forward in Dr. Greg Bogart's treasure of a series on therapeutic astrology.

—Claudia Bader, PhD, NCGR-PAA Level IV Counseling Astrologer

This is a short but comprehensive manual on how astrology can guide both the psychotherapist and the patient through times of great emotional crisis, using the patient's horoscope and current transits. The writing is such that any intermediate astrologer can easily see the reflection of the client's life in the horoscope, where we can swiftly identify the indicators of a troubling issue or occurrence. How much more difficult it must be for psychotherapists who are just beginning to know a client after many sessions. If they only knew what astrology could do!

—Barbara Ybarra, author of *Emotional Dimensions of Astrology*

My heart is filled with appreciation for the depth of wisdom and clarity of purpose Greg expresses in his new work. He shows that the practice of humanistic astrology oriented toward therapeutic consultation encourages enlightenment, empowerment, healing and evolution. I have utilized a humanistic, therapeutic approach in my astrology consultations with clients for many years and have observed first-hand how healing can be accelerated and enhanced using this model. Psychological patterns are brought into focus quickly, and we can see the horoscope as an overview of where the soul is trying to grow. Each example in Greg's book illustrates in practical terms how astrology can be utilized for profound transformation.

—Kathy Rose, Roseastrology.com

Greg Bogart's brilliant new text explores the dynamics of psychotherapy through an astrological lens. It describes for the reader how to walk the mystical path with practical feet. Greg's research effectively demonstrates the clinical importance of integrating astrology with psychological counseling.

—Dennis M. Harness, Ph.D.
President Emeritus of the American College of Vedic Astrology

With this volume, Greg Bogart continues to demonstrate why he is one of the premier therapeutic astrologers working today. Mental health professionals are offered the opportunity to witness astrology being therapeutically applied and astrologers will be inspired as to how they may deepen their practice to increase their effectiveness. Bogart writes in a crisp and practical style with case examples conveying human dynamics with clarity while undergirded by solid psychological theory and archetypal astrology. You hold in your hands a rare gem of a book.

—Brad Kochunas, M.A., Clinical mental health counselor and author of
The Astrological Imagination

This well-written, inspiring book is a great contribution to the field. Greg Bogart shares his knowledge and insight through case studies that illustrate the combined use of astrological and therapeutic techniques to foster healthy changes in his clients. His accounts raise the bar on the practice of astrology, and demonstrate that people can experience lasting growth and evolution in their lives and relationships.

—Cathy Coleman, Ph.D., Astrologer and Author of *Intrepid Explorer: Reflections on the Life and Legacy of Ralph Metzner*

Greg Bogart continues to demonstrate his mastery of combining astrology and psychotherapy. For students and professionals alike, this book is a must read, the quintessential guide to healing difficult relationship patterns with therapeutic astrology.

—Gisele Terry, M.A., Astrologer and Marriage and Family Therapist

Through his writings over the years, Greg Bogart has offered his readers insightful ways to navigate the therapeutic and astrological waters so that they feel more able to approach client work with discernment and positive intention. His newest publication is a treat for the professional and upcoming astrological consultant and an important contribution to our field.

—Frank Clifford, Principal of the London School of Astrology

Greg is that rare person who is genuinely both a psychotherapist and an astrologer, thus his thoughts on how the two disciplines can serve each other hold great value. As an experienced practitioner who has helped many people, we should take seriously his thoughts on how astrology and psychology complement one another. Those of us who have practiced psychotherapy and astrology know that this is a powerful combination that can rapidly unpack peoples' process of transformation.

—Mark Jones, author of *The Soul Speaks*

This book is a tour de force of good interpretation, without recourse to exotica or the assumption of prior knowledge. It is deceptively simple in its sound, basic approach, yet eloquent, indeed profound in its grasp of how transits actually work in the real world. Bogart's skill is brought home especially in his grasp of slow planet combinations in hard aspect, which many astrologers find confounding. He does blue ribbon work disguised as everyday bread and butter.

—Ken Bowser, author of *An Introduction to Western Sidereal Astrology*

Greg's latest book is a captivating exploration of the profound insights achievable through a humanistic approach to astrology in a therapeutic context. With heartfelt narratives from his transformative healing work with clients, he unveils the boundless potential of uniting astrology with psychological exploration. Greg stands as a stalwart guardian, preserving one of the 20th century's most significant astrological contributions: humanistic astrology. This approach not only serves as an invaluable tool for embracing life's fullness but also unveils a portal into our co-creative processes, fostering heightened awareness of the cosmic forces conspiring to aid our growth. Greg's work illuminates this often untapped potential within astrological counseling. In addition, Greg's work shows us how astrology can offer valuable perspective regarding the stages of our personal development as we age and evolve, with the planets marking time in predictable ways along our journey. Greg also illuminates the capacity of modern astrology to transcend the confines of antiquated astrological descriptions, which often prove overly negative, restrictive, and even detrimental. This message carries paramount importance within the astrological community, especially in the midst of a renaissance in interest for ancient forms. Greg's work is a powerful testimony to the personal journey of healing and growth accessible to all of us who seek wisdom through observations of the cosmos and our interconnectedness with it.

—Tony Howard, founder of Astrology University

Astrology as a Therapeutic Art
Healing Human Relationships

Greg Bogart, PhD, MFT

THE WESSEX ASTROLOGER

Published in 2024 by
The Wessex Astrologer Ltd
PO Box 9307
Swanage
BH19 9BF

For a full list of our titles go to
www.wessexastrologer.com

© Greg Bogart 2024
Greg Bogart asserts his moral right to
be recognised as the author of this work

ISBN 9781916625037

Cover artwork 'Temple of Healing' © Patricia Bowers
Design by Fiona Bowring at Bowring Creative
Typesetting by Kevin Moore

A catalogue record for this book is available at The British Library

No part of this book may be reproduced or used in any
form or by any means without the written permission of the publisher.
A reviewer may quote brief passages.

Table of Contents

Preface	vii
1. Astrology and Psychotherapy: A New Synergy	1
2. Astrological Relationship Counseling: Nine Vignettes	13
3. Astrotherapeutic Interventions	43
4. Relationships in Transition: Pathways of Change	59
5. Concluding Thoughts	95
Acknowledgments	101
References	103

Preface

The first astrologers were priests of the ancient Near East who discovered a cosmic order in the heavens. They invented writing, mathematics, and precise observation of the heavens. I believe now, 5000 years later, it is time for astrologers to assume a more respected role in our present culture by demonstrating how celestial observation can enhance our wellbeing, our mood and outlook, our positive embrace of others, and our optimal adaptation to life.

The current transit of Neptune in Pisces supports the study of astrology alongside mythology, dreams, and creative imagination, but Neptune also represents the experience of suffering. In 2021–22 transiting Jupiter and Neptune in Pisces brought new waves of human suffering emanating from a global pandemic, devastating warfare, berserk shootings, and intense social and environmental upheavals. At the same time, human relationships are strained and frayed. Neptune in Pisces invites us to cultivate compassion, to become instruments of *metta*, loving kindness, empathy, as well as higher intuition. In 2023–24 Saturn joins Neptune in Pisces, representing heightened awareness of human suffering, and an emphasis on social service, humanitarian relief, and, for some of us, a focus on treatment of problems such as clinical depression, a topic I've explored in several publications.[1] Saturn's approaching 2025 conjunction with Neptune (in the first degrees of Aries) creates in me an urge to show astrology's great value for our collective mental health. With this transit we're entering a period when we can ground the esoteric and the visionary, and I hope to do this by showing astrology's practical utility in relieving human suffering.

In previous works (*Therapeutic Astrology*, *Planets in Therapy*, and *Astrology's Higher Octaves*) I've described how I came to practice therapeutic astrology, an approach that combines celestial symbolism, depth psychology, and the psychology of human development in pursuit of emotional and psychological wholeness. This book briefly restates some core astrotherapeutic principles, but my main purpose here is to demonstrate how astrology can help us evolve a deeper understanding of our human relationships, through a series of examples—stories of relationship conflicts, quandaries, impasses, romance, rupture, and reconciliation. I describe how astrology shines a light on interpersonal discord and emotionally vulnerable situations and facilitates safe passage to new stages of conscious life.

This book assumes the reader is already familiar with basic astrological symbols and the meaning of planets, zodiacal signs, houses, and the study of transits and progressions. Utilizing these fundamentals, I detail examples of how an astrologer works to understand the dynamics of human interactions, encompassing spousal, parent-child, sibling, and employer-employee relationships. Rather than emphasizing synastry (chart comparison) and composite charts, I focus on delineating the individual charts and the challenges and tasks each person is facing as a means to heal and harmonize relationships. These examples illustrate the power astrology has to transform consciousness and behavior in the relational sphere, enhancing our lives in the home and workplace.

Chapter 1

Astrology and Psychotherapy: A New Synergy

In this book I explore the synergistic union of astrology and psychotherapy, which generates a potent force field for change within the personality. I discuss what it means to approach astrology therapeutically, for emotional healing and positive behavioral change. There are many forms of psychotherapy, so what I offer here are some examples of the specific ways I personally do this work. I describe how I combine astrology and professional mental health care in the hope of inspiring future practitioners to pursue the calling to this occupational path. I begin with a few thoughts on the past and future of therapeutic astrology.

A hundred years ago Jung talked about the psychological value of astrology and he used it to understand the compatibility of married couples. Decades later Stephen Arroyo developed those insights through his work as a Marriage and Family Therapist, one of the first people to successfully integrate astrology into a professional psychotherapy practice and to write about it. Dane Rudhyar developed humanistic, person-centered astrology emphasizing choice, free will, self-actualization, and the distillation of spiritual meanings from each experience. James Hillman and Stan Grof touted the power of astrology's archetypal symbolism, and Liz Greene and Karen Hamaker-Zondag reimagined astrology in the light of Jungian psychology. Zipporah Dobyns applied psychological theories to chart interpretation and the analysis of character in her masterwork, *Expanding Astrology's Universe*.[2] Noel Tyl explained astrology in terms of psychological concepts, beginning with description of the Moon as symbol of a person's reigning needs. In his book *Holistic Astrology*,[3] Noel described how he used astrology to address psychological ailments and for remediation of problematic behaviors. More recently, psychologist Michael Mayer described the integration of astrology into clinical practice in his book *The Mystery of Personal Identity*, describing astrology as "a language of personality."[4]

When I first began to study astrology, I was inspired by Rudhyar's student, Dr. Alex Ruperti, who gave a comprehensive presentation of planetary cycles and their psychological meaning. I was particularly struck by this passage:

> [C]hange necessarily involves crises. . . . . A crisis, however, is not a terrible calamity. A crisis is a turning point — that which precedes change. . . . [T]o humanistically oriented astrologers, crises . . . , both large and small, are essentially opportunities for growth. . . . Some of these turning-points are biological (such as adolescence and menopause) and are met at specific ages, while others are individual and may occur at any time during the life-span. . . . An astrologer can deduce the timing and nature of potential future crises from the transits and progressions. . . . The humanistic astrologer should know . . . that crises are not isolated events, but phases of individual growth. He should interpret them with reference to the smaller or greater cycles within which they occur—as phases of these cycles. The phase to which the crisis corresponds will reveal its meaning and purpose in terms of the nature, scope and purpose of the cycle as a whole. Humanistic astrology will therefore be able to bring a sense of direction, orientation and purposefulness to every crisis. The ability to envision what could and should develop in the future (i.e., the aim and purpose of the complete cycle) even while one is in the midst of a chaotic current situation . . . must be learned by facing

experiences in terms of the fourth dimension of time—that is, by seeing the whole cycle in every living moment and by approaching that present moment in a clear and conscious manner.[5]

This was meaningful when I first read it because I was going through a crisis with transiting Neptune conjunct natal Saturn. I was traveling around with a backpack without a sure direction, a dandelion in the wind. With the understanding astrology provided, I was able to cross a threshold in my life and come through it feeling whole, centered, and more psychologically organized. This was the origin of my interest in approaching astrology therapeutically.

When I started out as an astrologer, I had no training at all in counseling skills. And I discovered that clients frequently brought up issues I wasn't trained to handle or navigate. I didn't know what to do when a client was despondent or reported suicidal thoughts or revealed they were a survivor of incest, or struggled with a drug addiction, or had a very complicated family situation. When I was a 25-year-old astrologer, a female client began crying and regressed in my presence to the emotional state of a frightened child. How should I handle these situations?

I'd been reading charts for 7 years when I started grad school in counseling psychology during my Saturn return. I began studying astrology at the waning square of Saturn, but at my Saturn return I was trying to set a more sound foundation for my livelihood. During internships I'd often look at the client's birth dates listed on their intake forms, and even if we never discussed astrology I'd follow transits to a client's birth chart (or noon chart) and think about their situation in that light, as a background reference point. I could see that what was happening in their life was synced to astrological influences, and this helped me guide the counseling process. I observed changes occurring in a person over time and how it was linked to planetary cycles. And I began to view charts more through the lens of assessment, personality theory, developmental psychology, and the study of family systems. As an astrologer who was used to talking a lot in sessions, I had to learn greater capacity for empathic listening, a key feature of psychotherapy. I learned the art of bringing to someone's attention the self-defeating ways they engage in denial, rationalization, or projection—and learned to gently confront these defenses in a way that isn't wounding and doesn't drive the person away. I described my approach to astrotherapy, with many case examples, in *Therapeutic Astrology*, published in 1996 with transiting Uranus entering Aquarius, and later in *Planets in Therapy* and *Astrology's Higher Octaves*. I've become convinced that astrology can play an essential role in psychotherapy and can act as a potent antidepressant, possibly better than Prozac. It can be a key component of a holistic approach to mental health care, combined with dreamwork, meditation, and somatic disciplines such as hatha yoga, dance, and tai chi. And while astrology hasn't yet gained wide acceptance by psychologists, I firmly believe this synthesis is the wave of the future, the future that is now, with Pluto entering Aquarius.

Pluto in Aquarius represents evolution of a more progressive social consciousness, and a focus on alignment with groups that work for positive social change. It's a time when organizations and professions are changing and adapting. I can envision a future where many psychotherapists routinely utilize astrology in their work. We just need enough skilled astrologers to get trained and licensed as mental health professionals so legally we can call ourselves therapists or counselors, and then demonstrate in practice and in published case studies the spiritually meaningful outcomes that are possible by combining planetary symbolism with therapeutic methods.

Psychotherapy is enhanced by astrology's rich archetypal symbolism and its precise timing and awareness of how time is organized. The birth chart's detailed portrait of our potentials provides the ultimate roadmap for therapy, which seeks actualization of that potential. It's a marriage made in heaven. Practicing astrology therapeutically in ongoing sessions spread over time, as opposed to a single session of astrological counseling, allows us to work things through more deeply and to focus on the overall arc of learning that occurs over the course of a transit or a long progressed aspect.

In therapeutic astrology, we study the birth chart and transits to understand emotional dynamics and recurring themes of a life, to construct a cohesive self-narrative, and to identify traumas, stressors, and developmental tasks. We study the natal Sun—its sign, house, and aspects—for self-understanding, as Sun is the focal point of identity. By studying the natal Moon's sign, house, and aspects to other planets we gain insights into our emotional life, our abiding moods, our primary needs. Further goals are to integrate various subpersonalities and achieve psychosynthesis. This approach to astrology tries to clarify the meaning of passages or crisis a person is passing through. We gain understanding of stressed phases of relationships in the light of transits to the Descendant or through the 7th house. Astrology helps us see possibilities for the future so we can begin to do something to improve our situation. We believe that our state of wellbeing and mental health can be positively affected through attunement to nature's cycles and phases, shown by celestial patterns. We can utilize astrological knowledge for therapeutic self-examination and self-guidance, and it can also become a steady reference point for those who work as helping professionals.

In my previous writings I've described therapeutic astrology as *dialogical*, *process-oriented*, and *developmental*. Therapeutic results emerge from *dialogue*, from asking questions that allow the person to tell their story, so we can feel how the chart is resonating. In contrast to those who approach astrological sessions as a kind of psychic reading, we can approach the work as a dialogue that will evoke spontaneous discoveries of meaning in the course of counseling sessions. We honor the spontaneity of the interpretive moment and follow where the process leads.

Process Orientation in Therapeutic Astrology

In therapeutic astrology we can focus on a problem or dysfunctional behaviors, and allow the chart to spark insights that help us work through the problem. Laurie, who had an Aquarius Moon exactly quincunx a Mars-Uranus conjunction in Cancer in her 7th house, experienced many breakups, as she often felt suffocated and repeatedly bolted from relationships. We identified a pattern that whenever a man shows needs or exhibits clinginess she immediately breaks up with him. This response was maladaptive, unhelpful. It didn't allow any deeper attachment to form and she felt the loneliness of that. And she judged herself that she seemed incapable of forming a union with somebody. The boyfriend would become needy and insecure and needed a hug or other reassurance of their connection, in line with the symbolism of the sign of Cancer, which represents the urge for secure attachment and bonding. That's when Laurie became irritated and would reject the attachment-seeking behavior, the man would feel rejected and became cranky and angry, and then she'd suddenly end the relationship. Then she felt depressed and realized she missed the sexual fire of Mars-Uranus. Her Moon in Aquarius quincunx Mars-Uranus seemed to signify avoidant attachment style, where we exhibit a false self-sufficiency and put up defenses against future injury by acting aloof, like we don't care, we don't need anybody.

In adopting a therapeutic frame, I draw on insights of the great psychologist James Bugental. Bugental said that some core assumptions of existential-humanistic psychotherapy are that the capacity to deal with a life concern exists within the person having that concern, and a person comes to therapy because of an impaired ability to use their latent resources in dealing with the concern, to act to reduce that concern so that life will be different and better. Bugental taught that the primary means to overcome the blocks to access to one's own resources is *inward searching*, a practice related to meditation, creative thinking, prayer, and contemplation, where we describe the concern as fully as possible, keeping open to whatever feelings or insights present themselves.[6] This is where asking questions and giving the client room to free associate is so important.

I asked Laurie about her family, as Mars in Cancer sometimes indicates an inflamed clan or domestic situation, and she described her parents' volatile marriage and how her father ultimately left the family to escape his wife's rage. Now in her adult life it seemed that whenever a man became needy or whiny or angry or pleaded for more emotional connection Laurie acted like her abandoning father and quickly bailed from the situation. She suddenly gained a new insight about her rationale for abruptly ending relationships. Subsequently, Laurie worked to change this behavior and become more tolerant of the insistent emotional demands she could expect from Mars in Cancer in her 7th house. At the same time, with her Aquarius Moon and Uranus on the Descendant, for a relationship to work out, she knew she needed to maintain some degree of independence, and while her progressed Moon passed through Cancer and her 7th house she established a relationship where she and her boyfriend continued to live separately rather than cohabiting. They'd meet, have a great time for a few days, then return to their own homes, and they were both satisfied with that arrangement. She realized she didn't need to be in a traditional marriage, even though her parents disapproved. She saw that one of her spiritual lessons in this lifetime is to allow a relationship partner to be emotional and passionate and to depend on her. These insights emerged through our process-oriented approach to the symbolism. This was in contrast to her previous experience with astrologers who told her that her Mars in Cancer was in its fall (opposing Capricorn, Mars's sign of exaltation), and that her Mars was weak. Our process exploration of Mars in Cancer framed this placement as the need to evolve her capacity for secure attachment.

Therapeutic Astrology's Developmental Emphasis

Astrology is the study of our continuing evolution over time. We observe how each moment is a meaningful phase of a larger cycle and cycles of development. Therapeutic astrology is informed by a developmental perspective, as it describes our movement through time and suggests paths to developing many faculties and facets of the self, as we evolve our expression of each planet, our embodiment of each archetype. In *Planets in Therapy*, I map out how various planets are linked to developmental lines, stages, and milestones detailed by psychologists. For example, Mercury is linked to our cognitive development, evident in evolution of speech, language, and communication skills, and during periods when this planet is activated and accentuated we can sharpen our ability to consciously deploy and direct our attention. On a few occasions I've seen stressful aspects to Mercury manifest in attention deficit or disabilities affecting learning, reading, or speech. Similarly, the Moon is our key to understanding our emotional development and overall mood and demeanor, hence its importance to therapeutic astrologers.

In my work I often refer to Erik Erikson's model of development across the lifespan, which asserts that we gradually achieve eight core capacities: trust, autonomy, initiative, industry, identity, intimacy, generativity, and ego integrity. With a developmental lens we can assess when someone is struggling with one of the core tasks—for example if a person is mistrustful, unduly dependent, unmotivated, unproductive, confused about identity, isolated, bored and stagnant, or full of regret. Then we can try to address the problem.

Our first milestone during infancy is to achieve a feeling of trust that our needs will be met by caregivers—trust that I'm safe, protected, and my basic needs satisfied, so I'm able to trust others going forward, and trust life to provide what I need. Otherwise, I become wary, mistrustful, and inhibited. For astrologers, this baseline state of emotional health is linked to the condition of the natal Moon. My understanding of the Moon and its sign of Cancer is informed by John Bowlby's attachment theory, which describes our need throughout life for secure attachment. We feel safe, comforted, and inwardly serene when we're connected to, or in the proximity of, caregivers and loved ones. That's how we establish a secure feeling of trust in life, trust in others. If the natal Moon is stressed and our attachment is insecure in infancy or childhood, if we can't reliably get our basic needs fulfilled by caregivers during infancy and childhood, then patterns of insecure attachment form and may continue into adulthood, evident either in avoidant behavior or aggressive, ambivalent behavior. For example, some Moon-Uranus aspects show a tendency toward avoidant attachment style, where we act aloof, as if we aren't available, aren't interested, we don't need anybody, exhibiting extreme self-sufficiency. That used to be me. We also saw this with Laurie's Aquarius Moon quincunx Uranus. If the Moon is stressed by hard aspects to Pluto or Mars a person may develop an insecure-ambivalent attachment style, where relationships feature a great deal of anger, aggression, or lashing out at others to punish them in response to unmet needs, as a defense against the threat of abandonment. I'll illustrate this later.

Psychologically-oriented astrologers also note the developmental role of Mars. In Erikson's model, the next two challenges in early childhood are to achieve autonomy and initiative, both linked to Mars. At the first Mars return at age 2, children, unless they have a disability, typically develop *autonomy*. We gain the ability to stand, walk, and act independently, to exercise our will; otherwise we remain dependent on others, lacking confidence, full of shame and self-doubt. During preschool years, especially emergent near the second Mars return at age 4, we ideally see emergence of *initiative*, a sense of purpose, motivation, and goal-directedness. We learn to kick a ball into a goal or hit the ball and run and reach home plate, or run fast toward the finish line, or tag the other kids. At subsequent Mars transits, hopefully we're able to fire our engines and get motivated. In certain cases stressful aspects or transits involving Mars manifest in lack of motivation and vitality, impulsiveness and misdirected energy, overactive or underactive libido, and problematic expressions of anger. More on this later.

We must also consider the developmental importance of Saturn, which enables us to gain some degree of self-control over our instinctual Mars fire. Most astrologers are aware of how the four main phases of the Saturn transit cycle correlate with normative stages of development in childhood, adolescence, and adulthood. For example, during middle childhood and elementary school years, beginning at our first Saturn square, ages 7–8, we enter the phase Erikson calls *industry* versus inferiority, focused on education, developing competency, learning skills (such as arithmetic, spelling, drawing), and completing tasks. This industrious, productive self-organization prepares us to be attentive students and later to become functional workers and social contributors. Otherwise we're burdened by feelings of inferiority. It bothers us and hinders us if we can't get things done and finish tasks on time. In this first key phase of Saturn's cycle, and again at the opposition at age 14–15 and the age 22 waning square, and at every subsequent phase, our task is develop the personality traits associated with Saturn, which are broadly characterized as *conscientious*. From the perspective of the widely researched Five Factor Personality Theory, conscientiousness refers to self-discipline, competence, a sense of order, dutifulness, achievement striving, deliberation, and self-control. These traits are considered predictive of achievement, advancement, and success in work and career. For example, later I'll discuss the chart of Bailee, a young woman with Sun, Moon, and Mars in Virgo, trine Saturn in the 6th house. She's a Human Resources professional, and her chart immediately suggests that this is someone driven, motivated, meticulous, energetic, and capable of steady work performance. The presence or absence of the Saturnine, industrious, conscientious traits and behaviors substantially influence the course of our early and middle adulthood, when people take on responsibilities and make commitments to occupations and career paths, to friendships and relationships, marriage and family, developing a home, group affiliations, and creative pursuits, all of which require sustained effort over time.

Through attunement to Saturn we gain the focus and patience to complete high school, vocational school or college courses, or exhibit the steady reliability that enables us to hold a job. Therapeutic astrologers explain to clients that Saturn transits are maturational phases that challenge us to organize our time, our actions, and our life space. We track Saturn's transits through the houses, noting time periods of Saturn's key aspects to natal planets and horoscope angles. Natal Saturn's position establishes a persistent life theme, while transiting Saturn challenges us to reach specific milestones—for example, to work on consolidating our finances when Saturn transits the 2nd house, or to secure and maintain a good place to live when Saturn is in the 4th; or to develop a deeper interior spiritual life when Saturn transits the 12th house. Saturn in the 6th house represents a need to work on health issues and form healthy habits and routines. With Saturn in the 11th, we engage in group activity and commit to organizations or social movements. These themes give immediate focus to counseling, because Saturn's natal and current transiting placements indicate areas that need our sustained attention. Therapeutic astrologers try to help people meet the tests that Saturn poses for successful organization of life—in the home, in the realm of our occupations, in our intellectual life, artistic, and spiritual pursuits. And astrology's practical value is most evident in the insights it gives us that enhance our human relationships.

Chapter 2

Astrological Relationship Counseling: Nine Vignettes

Consulting astrologers advise clients facing a range of challenges in their relationships with spouses, friends, parents, and children. Planetary symbolism portrays both harmonious and discordant phases of life, helping us navigate the difficult periods so that hopefully relationships are sustained and renewed. In this chapter I'll describe some examples of how astrological work can aid our understanding of human relationships and evoke emotionally healing insights. We'll examine transits and progressions indicating key changes and evolution in spousal/marital, parent-child, sibling, and employer-employee relationships. I'll describe how, as a marriage and family therapist, I practice astrology therapeutically, in a way that's emotionally centered, process-oriented, and also strategic, focusing on tasks, intentions, and positive behavioral change. We'll look at how we can utilize astrology to form adaptive responses to the stressors that affect our interpersonal relations. Through these stories we gain appreciation for our common human predicaments and derive insights that we can apply to our own lives. At times the material is emotionally intense.

The basic organization of the chart begins with the Ascendant/Descendant axis, which represents consciousness poised between self and other, me and you. In the horoscope we have a map of the many spheres of life where relationships occur, not just 7th house friendship or marriage, but also 3rd house relationships with siblings, neighbors, roommates, schoolmates, and people we encounter or chat with in the course of daily life or in transit, or 11th house relationships we have within groups, teams, and organizations, or 6th house relationships with employees, trainees, coworkers, and health care providers. In the 10th house we maintain relationships with authority figures or bosses, or we ourselves are the boss or central leader or authority of an enterprise and learn to be in charge. Adding derived house analysis to the equation, we look at the 10th house as the 4th house from the 7th, thus governing the spouse or partner's family; similarly the 12th house is the 6th house from the 7th and represents the partner's health and workplace. The birthchart thus portrays a broad relational spectrum.

Some transits alert us to times of opportunity and developmental readiness to form relationships, for example during transits involving natal Venus, transiting conjunctions of Sun–Venus, Venus–Mars aspects, planetary transits through the 7th house or aspecting its dispositor, or aspecting natal planets in the 7th house. These are some typical indicators. Later I'll discuss how secondary progressed aspects reflect changing phases, cycles, and experiences of relationships. For example, Lynne, a busy professional woman who'd been putting zero energy into finding a boyfriend, had Saturn transiting through her 7th house at the same time as a transiting Venus-Mars conjunction in Capricorn, which seemed to indicate a threshold pertaining to friendship, partnership, or attraction. Lynne said a man named Brett had been showing a lot of interest in her, and that he was smart, dependable, caring, and easy to get along with. But she didn't think Brett was a serious prospect; the problem seemed to be that his hair was thinning and he was a little self-conscious about it. Otherwise he was adorable. As we discussed the meaning of the current transits she decided she might be willing to give this good, gentle, slightly balding guy a chance. They ended up forming a sweet relationship and became a couple. Lynne realized Brett's attention was worth her attention.

Besides alerting us to advantageous times for establishing new relationships, astrology helps us succeed in sustaining them. Each planet plays a role. Relationships are enhanced through Venus insofar as we express affection, when our behavior is agreeable, cooperative, and accommodating; when we're affectionate toward others. In personality theory, the traits of Agreeableness are considered key determinants of the success and harmony of relationships. Disagreeable, uncooperative, rigid and inflexible people have less rewarding relationships. The Sun is our identity, knowing who we are, and the capacity to acknowledge and validate the identity and individuality of another person, to express admiration. The Sun's radiance is expressed as extraversion, warmth, and enthusiasm. Mercury signifies communication and our willingness to engage in conversation and show curiosity about experience. Jupiter signifies tolerance, understanding, patience, generosity, integrity, pursuit of intellectual interests, ideals, and a quest for meaning. Saturn is the symbol of stability, consistency, reliability, and straightforwardness. And most importantly, Moon signifies affect attunement, attentiveness to another person's needs and feelings, and the capacity for secure attachment. Each person has their own emotional insecurities to work out to be capable of sustaining mutually satisfying relationships.

There are several planets that sometimes express or manifest in problematic behaviors that affect relationships—for example, Mars: anger, irritability, impulsiveness, conflict around expression of sexual drives; Uranus: distancing, defiance and noncompliance, irresponsible behaviors, the tendency to become overstimulated, jittery, and wired; Neptune: denial, delusional thinking, duplicity, addictions, relational victimization; Pluto: paranoia, domineering traits, festering resentment, explosive outbursts, emotional shutdown due to post-traumatic stress. Many astrologers think of these planets as malefic influences. The turn toward therapeutic astrology begins with the view that these planets can best be approached not as malefics but as *stressors*. There are always stressors in life, in our midst. There's always another transit of Mars and Saturn to look forward to. But it's possible to work consciously with these planetary energies and learn adaptive responses to stress. We'll return to this point. Watch especially for the key influence of Mars in my examples.

Wayne

Wayne was born on a Full Moon, with Sun and Moon square Pluto and Moon conjunct Mars in Scorpio. Wayne was referred to therapy for anger management after he became involved in several physical altercations in the workplace and his ex-wife got a restraining order against him after he got into jealous rages about her new boyfriend. His rude, argumentative behavior unsettled his relationships with people and some unpleasant

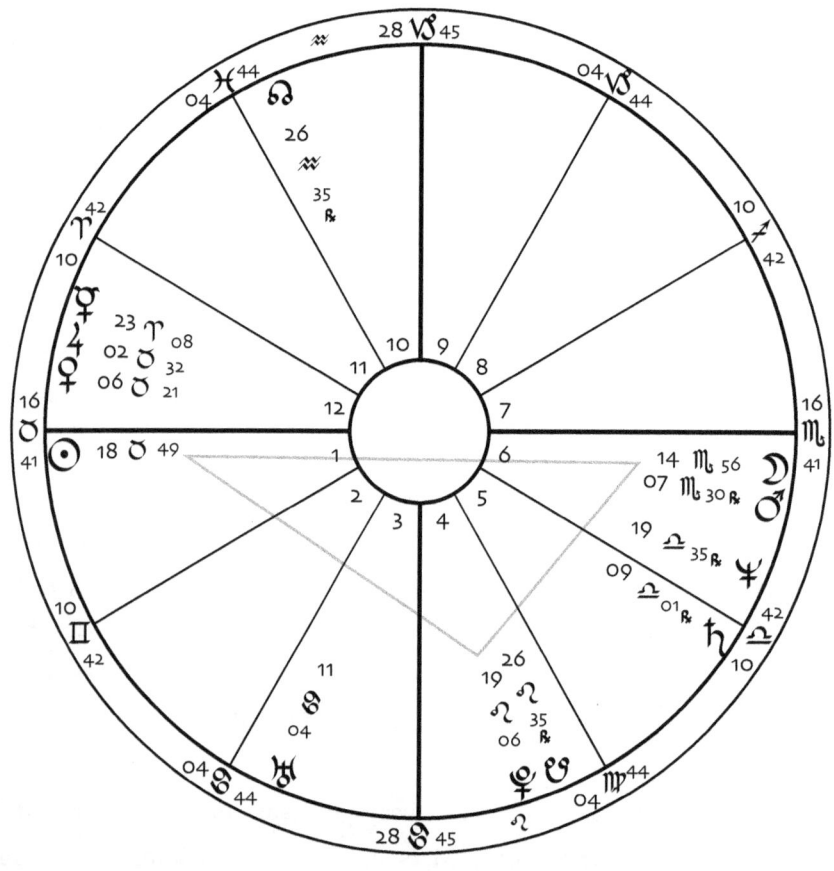

Wayne – May 9, 1952

incidents were timed by transits to the T-Square of Sun-Moon-Mars-Pluto. But it's not the planets that determine how our relationships evolve; it's our behavior. And it's possible to change our behavior. We have control over that, barring some physical or cognitive disability. Wayne came to understand that a family history of domestic violence (Pluto in 4th house) had been emotionally traumatic and caused him to become mistrustful and hostile toward others. He exhibited a high degree of angry hostility, which in personality theory is considered one of the neurotic, self-defeating traits. When transiting Saturn entered Aquarius and squared natal Mars, he resumed the discipline of weight lifting and focused his Mars energy on bulking up. And as Saturn squared his natal Moon at the Descendant Wayne had an emotional catharsis as he realized how much he'd always relied on his ex-wife and that he missed her profoundly. Soon thereafter he met a feisty, motorcycle-riding lady at the gym and started seeing her, and they've been getting along famously. He was able to turn a corner and begin a new phase.

Tina

Tina, age 69, showed me her chart, and the first thing I noticed was that transiting Pluto and Saturn were both squaring natal Mars in Aries in the 5th house, and solar arc Pluto had just two months earlier been exactly opposite natal Mars, from the 11th house. I asked if she was experiencing stress, conflicts, anger, and discord with a child, and she said she'd been estranged from her son John (age 50) for several months. He was angry at Tina for returning to school and felt his mother didn't give him enough attention. Apparently John's wife, Dorie, Tina's daughter-in-law, had been sending her angry, hateful, unpleasant emails and had screamed at Tina that she was crazy. By derived house analysis, the 11th house is the 7th house from the child 5th house and thus rules the child's marriage, the child's spouse. The combined energy of transiting Saturn and Pluto square Mars and solar arc Pluto opposite Mars evoked much negativity and discord.

Tina herself became enraged and screamed at John on several occasions. There was lots of anger and hurt feelings to process. Simultaneously, in June-July 2020 her solar arc Saturn was exactly square her natal Moon in Pisces, so she felt alone, rejected, emotionally fragile, and a bit sad. It was a difficult time of motherhood. It validated her experience to name these feelings in our session. But, I said, with Saturn square the Moon she could show emotional strength and maturity in seeing her son's behavior for what it was. She said, "He's acting like a two-year-old." A month after our initial meeting, Tina told me she'd felt so much relief since our conversation knowing that this big blowout was synced to these aspects involving Mars. She'd started developing her own Mars energy, her own vitality, by

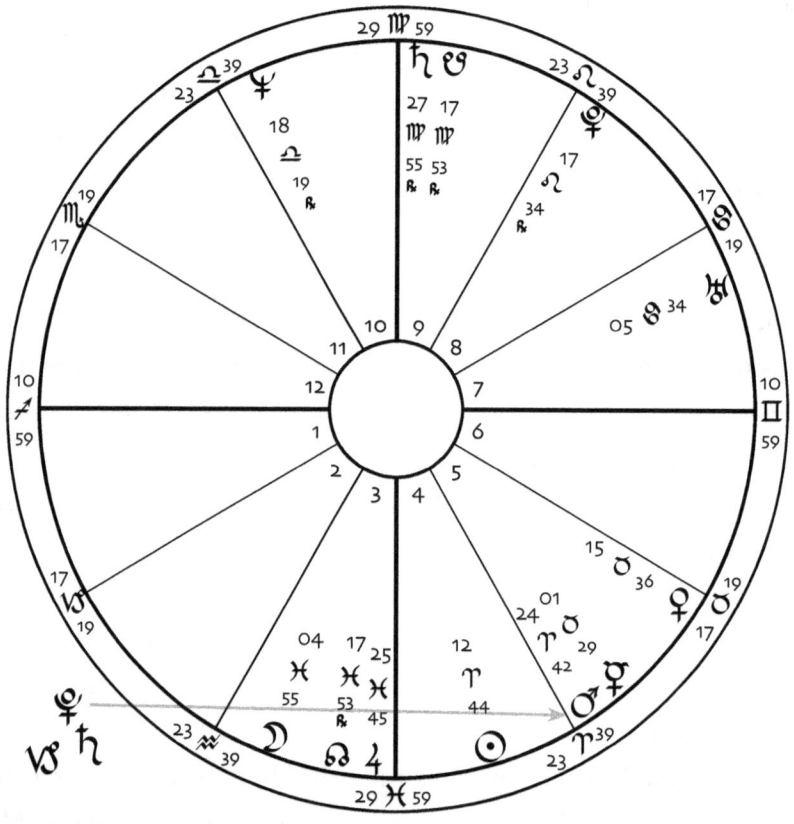

Tina – April 2, 1951

exercising and dancing. She also suddenly started getting attention from a man named Fred; after being solitary and unattached for the past 16 years, she felt a buzz of sexual energy and actually took the risk of signaling interest, and received an immediate response from Fred. She realized that she'd grown emotionally dependent on John since her husband died and that this Pluto transit to natal Mars in her 5th house represented a cutting of the emotional umbilicus. "I'll bet he was always a cranky boy," I said. "You got that right," she said. "Now he's Dorie's problem!" We both laughed. Her relationship with her son remained frayed for the time being but she was able to detach from him and rediscover her own exuberance. I was struck by how she experienced the contacts to Mars externally as

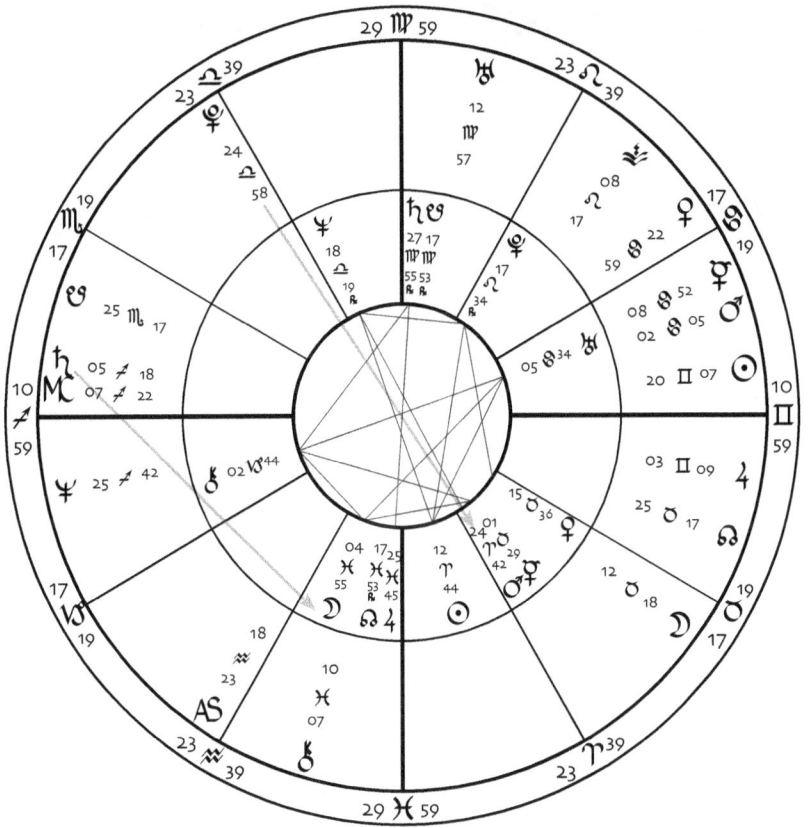

Tina – Inner wheel natal chart/outer wheel Solar Arc Direction, October 27, 2020

Astrology as a Therapeutic Art

discordant relations with the raging, temperamental John and his wife, but she was also able to experience Mars internally to exercise her will to live—and to play.

Alice

Alice has natal Moon in Cancer at the Midheaven and is very involved in her role as a nurturing mother of two boys, both of whom have severe learning disabilities (Mars in Pisces in 5th house). Alice was raised within a spiritual community and movement based in India and devotional yoga was the core of the practice (Venus-Neptune conjunction). With

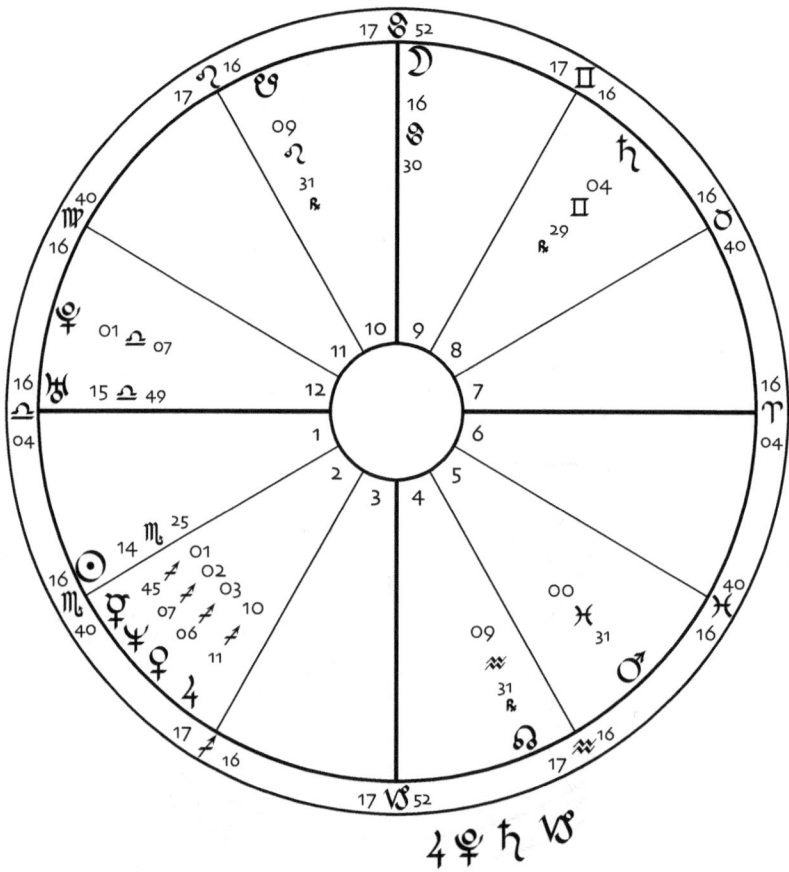

Alice – November 7, 1971

Mercury, Venus, and Jupiter conjunct Neptune she is deeply spiritual, with expansive philosophical, mystical interests. And since childhood Alice has spontaneously written poetry (Mercury-Neptune conjunction). "It comes out of nowhere," she says. But this Sagittarius stellium in her 2nd house also shows practical, material interests, and she informed me she is the chief financial officer of a corporation. The four Sagittarius planets opposed Saturn in the 8th house of business and shared finances; she manages a lot of other people's money and answered to investors and a board of directors. She negotiated financial agreements between organizations (Saturn in the 8th house of agreements and disagreements). I said, "This synthesis of the mystical and the financial is part of who you are. You don't have to pick one side or the other. These polar opposites are united in you."

I was interested in the fact that transiting Jupiter, Saturn, and Pluto had recently crossed her IC and were transiting her 4th house. She said that in March 2020, a few months earlier, she and her husband had purchased a house after renting for the past ten years, and over the summer they were quite involved with renovations and garden projects, all 4th house activities. But it struck me that there must be more to this transit of Saturn and Pluto in her 4th house and so I paused over it with her for a moment and asked if there'd been any recent revelations or disclosures related to the family, or any unpleasantness or resentment emerging with the family system. While she was establishing a more permanent base for her own nuclear family it occurred to me there might be something important surfacing within the larger clan. I mentioned that Pluto sometimes manifests in encounters with toxic emotions or people carrying a lot of negativity, resentments, or hostility toward others. I also wondered if this Saturn-Pluto transit in the 4th house might relate to some family adversity or bereavement. Alice replied, "My mom's second husband died recently and mom came back into my life after a long estrangement. My mother was somewhat physically abusive when I was a child. I recently called her out on it and we had a big blowup. This always needed to happen, and it happened and we survived it, the two of us. Then I became interested in our genealogy so we did a DNA test, and we discovered some buried secrets. It turns out my great grandfather abandoned his wife and kids and married another woman, had the same number of children with her, and gave all of them the exact same names as the first set of children—which seems weird and creepy. But in the process we discovered a whole new group of relatives I'm getting to know. Finding out these unsavory facts was unsettling but it allowed me to understand the secrecy I'd always sensed around my family history and the feeling that there were things that we don't discuss. There'd always been a sense of ancestral shame." And amazingly, Alice and her mother laughed and cried together at the tragedy and absurdity of her great grandfather's situation, and they bonded with each other in coming to terms with this buried family history. She said, "Talking about this now, I realize I've never in my life felt closer to my mother." All of this came to light through our discussion of transiting Saturn and Pluto in her 4th house, a time that was transforming her connection to family.

Amy

In the next example we'll see development of a new level of consciousness in response to secondary progressed aspects. Amy, age 35, recently separated from her husband in 2018 at the time of a progressed Full Moon, featuring a progressed Sun-Venus conjunction. The progressed Sun-Venus conjunction is often a significant indicator of love and marriage, and this could be regarded as its ultimate evolutionary goal. But in this case, the Full Moon closely squared her natal Mars and Pluto in Scorpio and Amy was rudely awakened when she discovered her husband's sexual infidelity. She expressed fierce anger as she exposed his deceit, but this ended up being a huge evolutionary step forward for her. She got fed up with his lies and excuses, hired a lawyer, and served him papers. She told me, "I kicked him to the curb in a major way."

Astrological Relationship Counseling: Nine Vignettes

Amy has a natal Sun-Neptune conjunction, with Venus nearby, and she's a very idealistic, mystical, and magical person, and she has repeatedly been a somewhat innocent victim in relationships, trusting and gullible, compliant, and several times deceived and disillusioned. This Full Moon squaring Mars and Pluto signified the emergent power and assertiveness to confront someone who hurt her; it brought a full venting of resentments between them and the realization of an irrevocable ending (progressed Sun and Moon square Pluto). The betrayed wife became the brave heroine who acted to rescue herself and become the commander of her own fate. Around this time Uranus transited into her 7th house, which showed change,

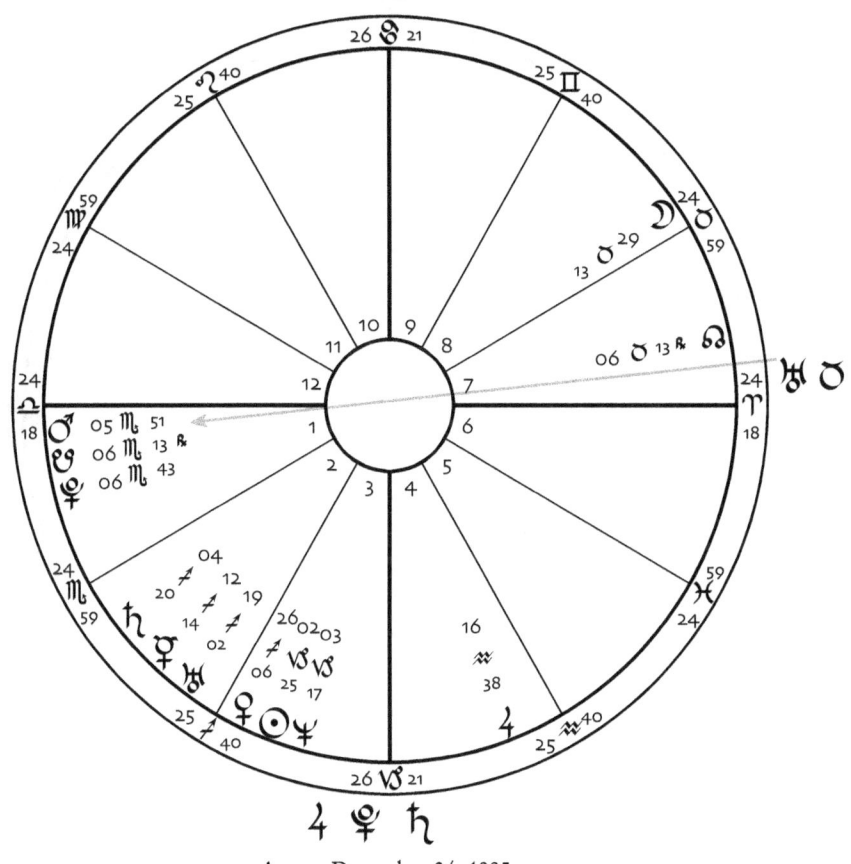

Amy – December 24, 1985

liberation, freedom, creating distance, differentiation from her husband; she was done being a victim. Transiting Uranus also opposed natal Mars and Pluto, further activating these planets. And when she left her husband she immediately got involved with a younger man, an I.T. genius, someone she considered to be exceptional. It happened really fast. All of her friends were shocked and couldn't believe she left her husband and immediately shacked up with somebody new. Her husband was devastated and said what she'd done was ruthless, that she was deliberately sticking it to him (Mars in Scorpio), and she couldn't deny it. Mars in the 1st house means that

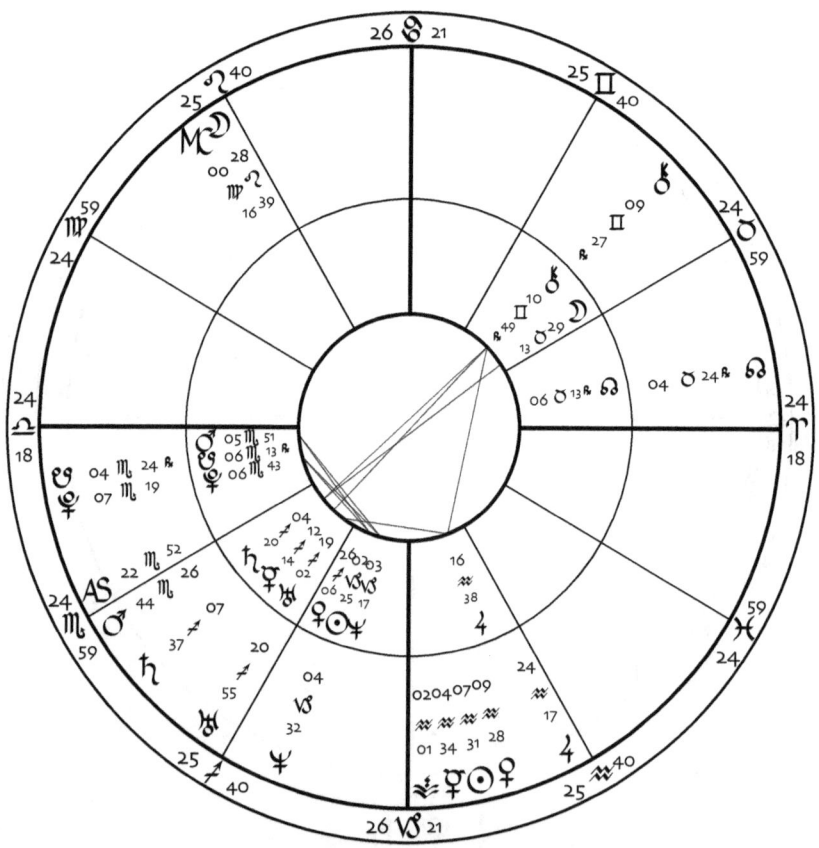

Amy – Inner wheel natal chart/outer wheel Naibod Secondary June 12, 2020

sometimes I have to act in a way that benefits my best interests. And that's what she did. This new couple set their marriage date to occur during the August 2021 Venus-Mars conjunction in Leo. A Venus-Mars conjunction is often a beautiful moment when people are more likely to meet, connect, pursue attractions, and experience passionate love. These conjunctions often mark the birth of new relationships, and in Leo, it was a time for celebrations. We're blessed that through this knowledge we can anticipate such a joyous moment. But the real value of astrology is that it illuminates not only the birth of love but also the many tests and challenges through which love is sustained over time.

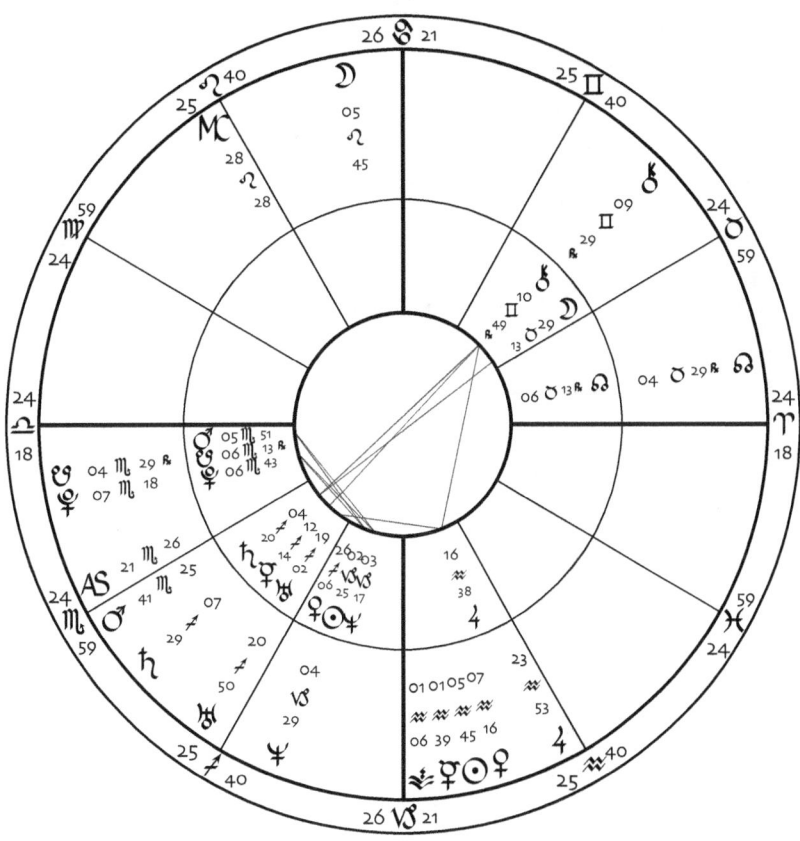

Amy – Inner wheel natal chart/outer wheel Naibod Secondary September 14, 2018

Mary

Look at the chart of Mary, who has Sun-Venus conjunction and owns her own business as a hair stylist. When I spoke to her, transiting Mars-Uranus had just reached conjunction in her 7th house, and the big shock in her marriage was that her husband Jake was recently diagnosed with terminal cancer. Since Uranus crossed her Descendant two years earlier she'd lost some friends and gained some new ones; she'd felt like she and Jake were growing apart and perhaps had outgrown each other, and she contemplated divorce. She had a sense that they were individuating from each other, but

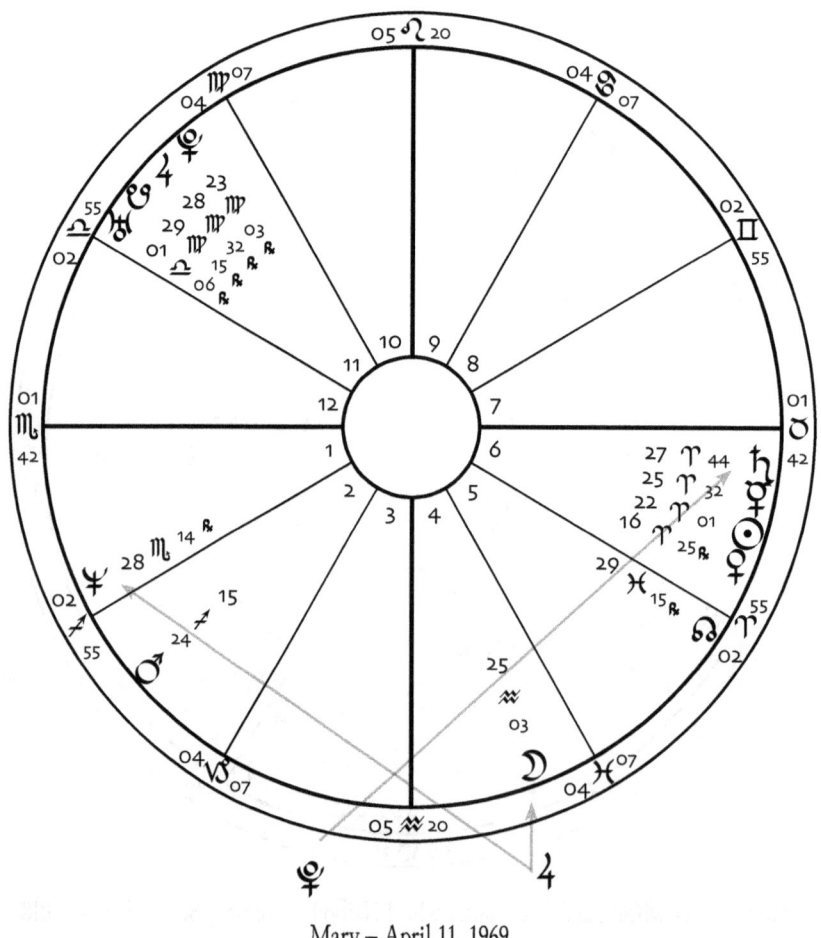

Mary – April 11, 1969

now that was playing out in a different way than expected, with Jake not expected to be alive much longer. Also, Neptune rules her 5th house and was transiting her 5th house in Pisces. I learned that for ten years her son Demian was a heroin addict, now a year in recovery (Neptune, planet of addictions, in the 5th house of children). Demian was a lost soul but had recently undergone a spiritual awakening and gone into treatment. Neptune is also the planet that can bring about an experience of redemption and grace. This was a huge blessing for her as she devoted so much of her financial and feeling resources to his wellbeing. With natal Jupiter-Pluto in Virgo she had a strong interest in energy medicine and herbology and she was trying to teach Demian how to draw energy from the earth and from food.

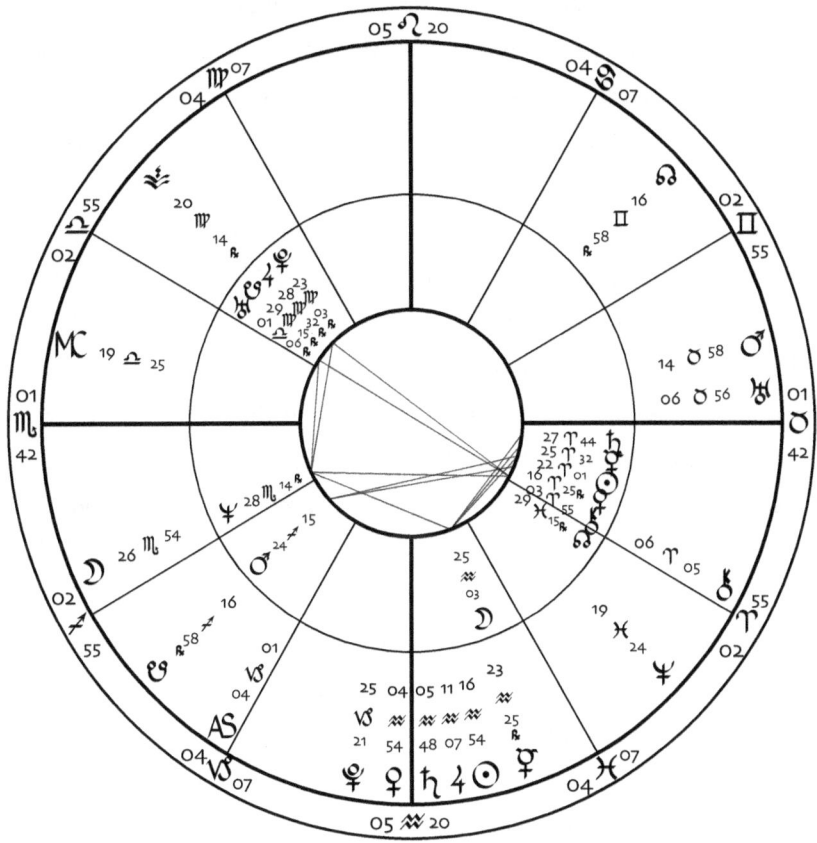

Mary – Inner wheel natal chart/outer wheel transits February 5, 2021

At the time of consultation, five planets were transiting Aquarius in Mary's 4th house and the whole family was pulling together around the crisis in Jake's health, especially Allan, of whom she said, "He's really there for us." Mary was also experiencing the support of an extended friend family and clan group. Transiting Jupiter was coming into conjunction with her natal Moon, square Neptune. Her path for this year was to be a compassionate caregiver, to feed and nurture Jake, to attend to him with devotion and selfless service, to soothe and comfort him. This was a choiceless choice, born of necessity. She kept nearby an image of Kuan Yin, bodhisattva of compassion, and thought about her often, striving to be her instrument. During this five-planet transit in her 4th house she reported that she'd been creating space outside for woodworking and she rearranged her art studio. Transiting Pluto was square Mercury–Saturn at her Descendant, and she found herself having frank and honest discussions with Jake about his condition, and his wishes. I mentioned that Pluto square Saturn can symbolize the feeling of losing the elder who is the rock and stabilizing force of one's life and the need to become, definitively, one's own father, in charge of oneself and one's destiny. Mary said, "Jake is actually 16 years older than me and his imminent passing is like losing my father." Mary also said that he was very pragmatic and straightforward, a practicing Buddhist, and that he was moving through this terminal diagnosis gracefully, to a place of acceptance, and without dramatizing it. Taking the situation more or less in stride, he was exhibiting a high degree of maturity, and was an incredible teacher for Mary, who strived to match his level-headedness. Knowing that transiting Pluto was approaching the square to natal Saturn allowed her to anticipate her next stage of development and maturation. She began to consider what the universe was intending and calling forth from her in the face of adversity and death itself.

Less obvious is the fact that Mary's natal Jupiter in the 11th house at 28° Virgo 32 was about to be aspected by a Saturn–Uranus square at 13 degrees of Aquarius and Taurus—both aspecting Jupiter by sesquiquadrate (135°), which could deepen her interest in broader social and environmental issues regarding health (Jupiter in Virgo), particularly trying to understand why people develop cancer (Jupiter conjunct Pluto). She said this was already a primary focus and a cutting edge of her learning.

It also occurred to me that she was experiencing transiting Pluto square Sun, Mercury, and Saturn in her 6th house, which is the 12th house from the husband 7th house. She was witnessing her husbanding perfecting his own spirituality by letting go, surrendering control, and seeking peace and enlightenment and awareness of his true identity transcending the physical body, the mind, memory, and imagination.

Note that I'm not focused on predicting when Mary's husband Jake will die. I'm there with her in the moment, in the center of the spectrum of emotions we experience when we, or our loved ones, are facing existential threats. I spoke to her again one year later and learned that Jake did indeed pass over peacefully during Pluto square natal Saturn. And Mary's life goes on.

Allen and Cathy

Here's the chart of Allen, a music producer, alongside the chart of his wife Cathy, who was recently named a partner in a big, fancy law firm. For several years, transiting Jupiter, Saturn, and Pluto in Capricorn were in Allen's 12th house, the house of spirituality, inner life, solitude, and being momentarily cloaked, invisible, behind the scenes. It's also the 6th house from the wife or spouse–7th house, so the 12th house signifies the partner's work, workplace, and health. Cathy was gone at the office every day and brought work home at night and on weekends. Totally focused on her legal work, she met the Capricorn tests of accomplishment, career mastery, and advancement, with flying colors. Transiting Jupiter-Saturn-Pluto were in her 10th house, and after several years of feverish, nonstop work and aggressive office politics and power struggles (while Pluto squared her natal Mars-Saturn-Pluto in Libra), she was finally elected a partner, as Saturn reached conjunction to natal Venus in her 10th house. Cathy's health had been strained for several years during the Saturn and Pluto squares to her natal Mars, Saturn and Pluto. She suffered from inflammation of joints, lower back pain (Mars-Saturn-Pluto in Libra, which rules the lumbar spine), and headaches—symptoms of pressure she was under in the workplace and the toll her stressful lifestyle was taking. It was also taking a toll on their marriage as she was often irate and belligerent during these transits to Mars-Saturn-Pluto in Libra. She needed better work/home balance and more time for exercise and leisure. Cathy continued her work from home during the pandemic, while Allen spent most of his time at home, caring for their daughter, working behind the scenes supporting his

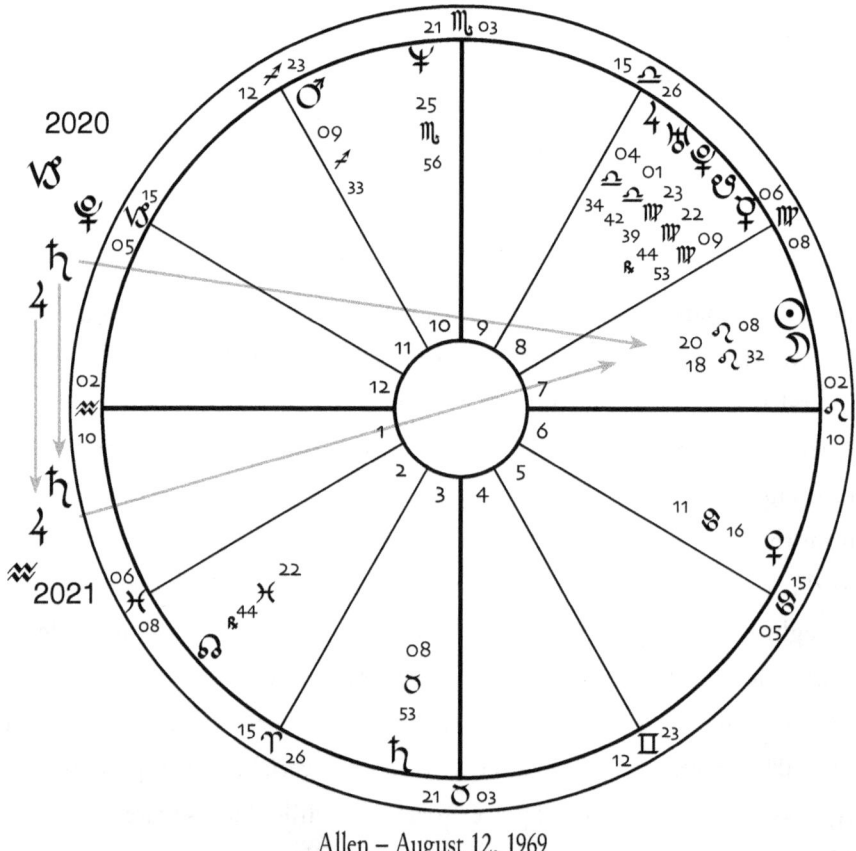

Allen – August 12, 1969

wife's occupational success. With three planets near her MC, Cathy's career was peaking, while Allen's career in the music business was at a low ebb. The 12th house is the house of karma and its results, and Allen continued to earn money from royalties for past works completed, and trusted the universe to provide. Cathy succeeded as the main breadwinner and he was the nurturing dad, and family cook, dishwasher, handyman, and gardener (Sun conjunct Moon). He didn't have a big outer world career during this period, but through the wisdom of astrology he learned to be okay with that. He meditated daily, trying to hold the peace for the household and for the good of the world.

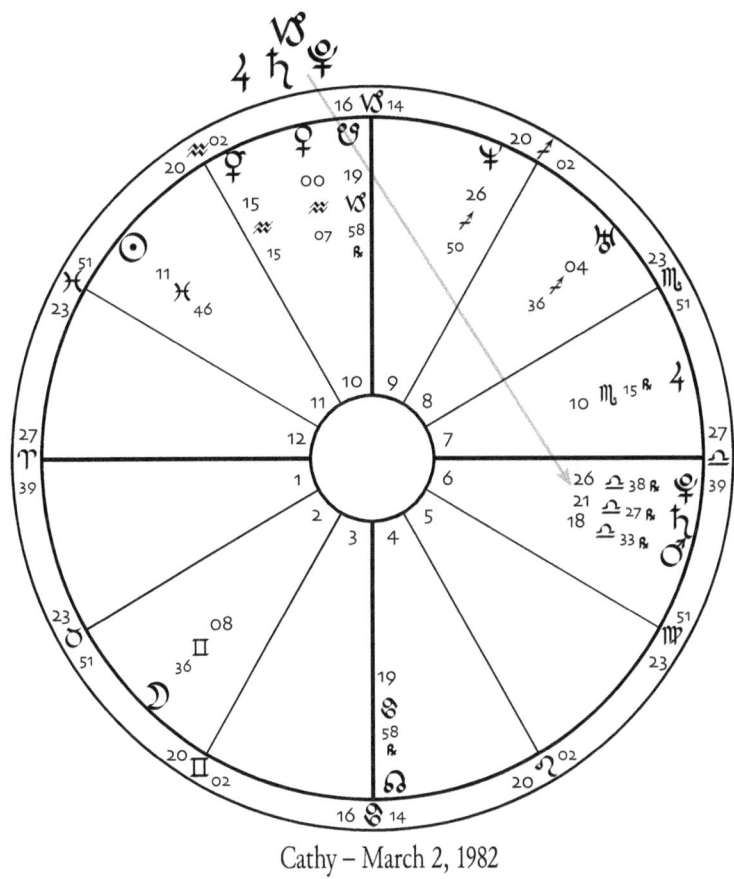

Cathy – March 2, 1982

Allen's knowledge of Cathy's transits helped him survive her frequent belittling comments and attacks and understand her physically and emotionally inflamed condition. Transiting Saturn and Pluto were quincunx his Sun and Moon for two years, signifying unpleasant quarrels, vindictiveness, and feeling cold, guarded, and separate from one another. Sometimes it felt like Cathy's disdainful words would destroy him. But Allen found the inner strength to endure her rages and contemptuous comments, which were mostly aimed at his reduced income. John Gottman says that criticism, contempt, defensiveness, and stonewalling erode trust and affection in marriage. What Allen did was try to minimize these tendencies in himself. We decided that he couldn't change Cathy. He could only try to improve himself, live the path indicated by his own chart, and let go of bitterness and resentments. Pluto quincunx Moon and Sun entailed a lot of injured pride, hurt feelings, and insults to the self, but he remained utterly focused on, and devoted to, his Leo queen and emotional dominatrix, making her the center of his attention, along with their daughter.

Recently transiting Saturn passed over Allen's Ascendant into the 1st house, a transit that often brings new decisions, responsibilities, and organizing priorities; and when transiting Jupiter in Aquarius opposed his natal Sun-Moon in Leo, Cathy gave birth to their second daughter. Allen and Cathy remained together as a couple through some very difficult transits and are now stronger and having more fun together than ever. And with transiting Uranus squaring the natal Moon and about to enter Allen's 4th house, they recently purchased a much larger house.

Ellen

Now look at the chart of Ellen, age 48, a divorced mother of two. With Sun sextile Jupiter in the 9th house of education, she has an administrative role in management of a large university. Her divorce occurred in the aftermath of a long transit of Pluto square her natal Mars-Uranus in Libra, the sign of marriage, which had unleashed much fury between Ellen and her husband Brian and a mutual desire for freedom and emancipation. As I further contemplated her chart, I noticed that many years earlier she'd had a progressed Venus-Mars conjunction, during the early days of the marriage, so, I said, this must have truly been a big love for her, a passionate romance. She and Brian truly loved each other. A transiting or progressed conjunction of Venus and Mars can be a time to find a loving and passionate union, but now she was on the other side of this. In relation to her recent divorce, I noted two relevant progressed aspects. Recently, in 2017–18, secondary progressed Mars was conjunct her Descendant. This corresponded to a time of constant arguing with Brian and the discordant conclusion of the

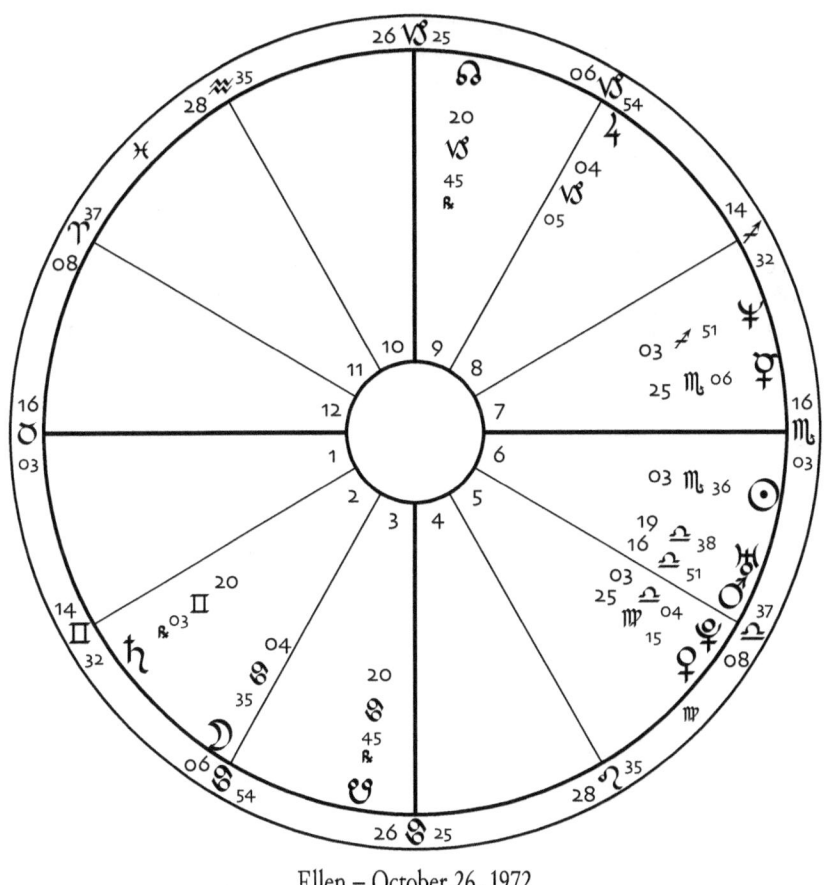

Ellen – October 26, 1972

Astrology as a Therapeutic Art

marriage as they definitively separated. She said he had a drinking problem and was always angry. It was powerful for her to realize how the atmosphere of the marriage had shifted so radically under the heat of progressed Mars on the Descendant. Also, from 2015–2019 Ellen had experienced progressed Sun opposite natal and progressed Saturn in the 2nd house. This span encompassed the period of alienation, separation, and divorce, when she had to get her financial house in order. I told her, "You kept the ship on course, created financial stability, did what you had to do; you held your university job, maintained a good home for your sons, and that was a great accomplishment." She teared up, feeling validated by this comment, and said it was a great relief to hear this. Now that progressed Mars had moved

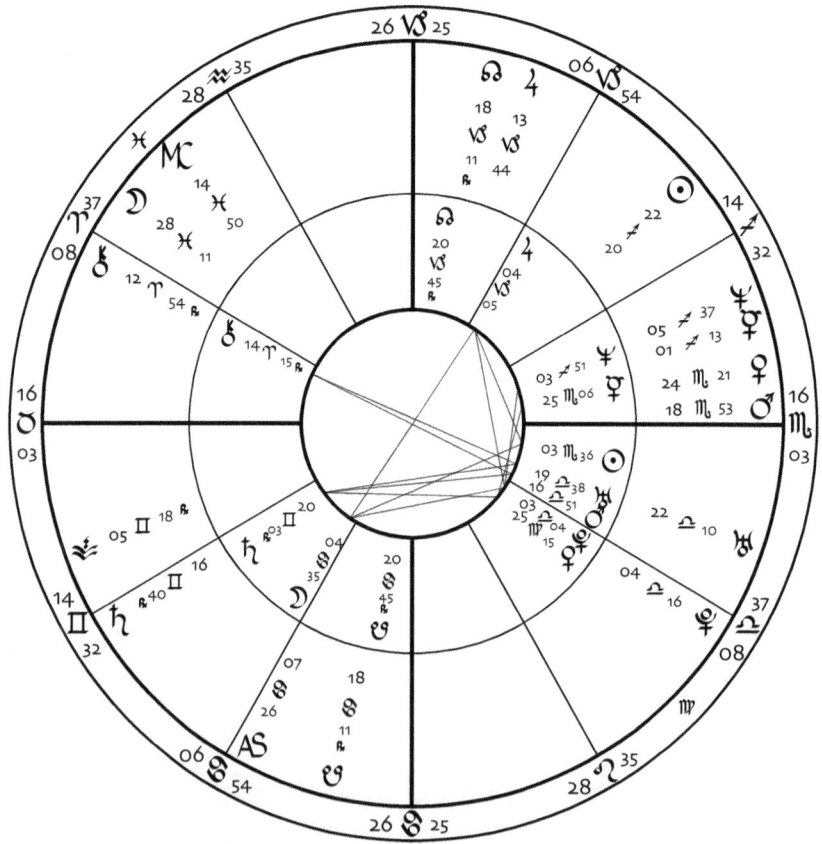

Ellen – Inner wheel natal chart/outer wheel Naibod Secondary February 15, 2021

away from her Descendant she and Brian weren't so angry with each other anymore and were becoming friends again. But she wasn't interested in returning to him or finding another relationship, not now at least. She'd had that experience and now it was over. We observed that the progressed Sun would square Venus in 2024, three years hence, so maybe then she'd feel ready to meet someone and start over, resuming a more relational focus. But that time was not now, and in this moment she had other tasks and other interests. With progressed Moon in the last degrees of Pisces she's experiencing loneliness and feeling her solitude intensely, as her teenage sons are increasingly self-sufficient and she's wondering how to redirect energy from parenting. She's devoting time to volunteerism, pitching in to help homeless people and local families in need. She feels drawn to solitude and spirituality with progressed Moon moving into her 12th house. And progressed Mercury is approaching conjunction with natal and progressed Neptune in her 7th house: She is seeking spiritual and intellectual friendships and has been studying books on metaphysics, mysticism, and astrology with her best girl friend, whom she views as her teacher. In this way she's following the path indicated by her planets to evolve herself through a new quality and focus of human relationship, less about passion and romanticism and more about spiritual companionship and development of the higher mind (Mercury-Neptune).

Louis

My next example is Louis, who was until recently a senior Vice President of a high-end fashion retail department store. His natal Venus, dispositor of the Taurus Sun, is semi-square the Sun, square Saturn, square Moon and Mars, sextile Pluto and could even be viewed as widely conjunct Jupiter. He is a fashion expert and visionary extraordinaire. From 2010–13 he had progressed Sun square Saturn in Aries in the 2nd house, and he moved into an executive position with huge responsibilities and a prodigious salary. He

Astrology as a Therapeutic Art

felt physically crushed by the long hours and the pressure to meet corporate expectations of huge profits.

A few years later, in 2016 Louis had progressed Sun square Mars in the 8th house of business and shared finances, credit and debt. He and his husband Randall became financially overextended, owning two homes and paying mortgages on both properties. "We were spending tons of money." He said Randall spent way too freely on extravagant clothes, furnishings, and lavish catered parties. All of this was before Covid hit. Then unexpectedly the company was sold in a corporate buyout and taken over by new management with whom Louis immediately clashed, and he decided to leave the company. Transiting Jupiter, Saturn, and Pluto were

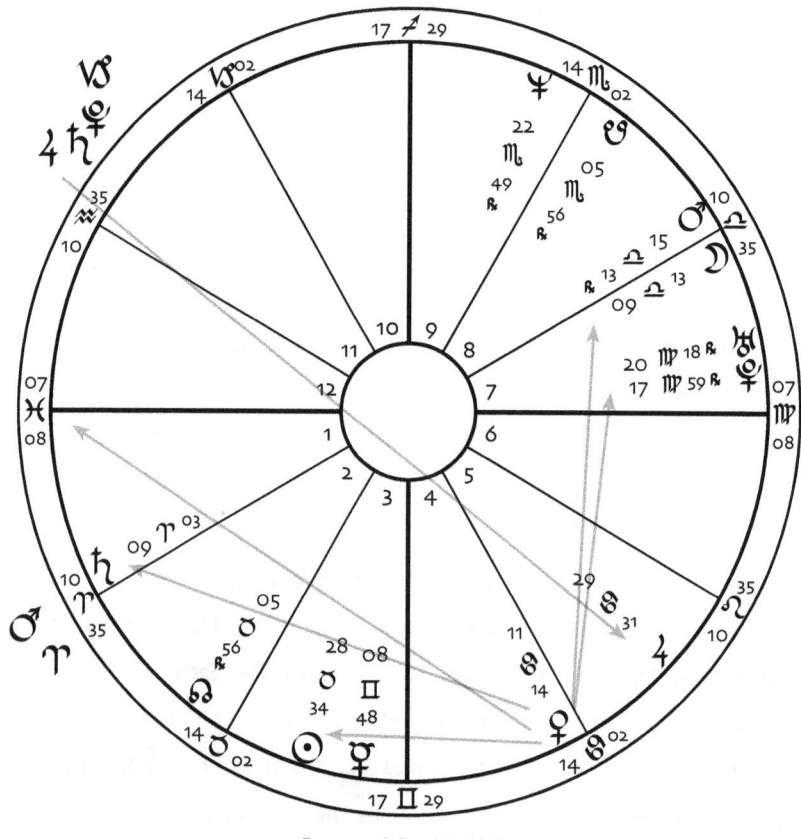

Louis – May 20, 1967

conjunct in Capricorn in his 11th house, which represents the team, the organization, the corporation.

He felt an immediate change in the company atmosphere and management style (Saturn and Pluto in Capricorn) and he no longer saw a place for himself in the new hierarchy. The problem was, he and Randall were holding all this debt, which was a major stressor, something he needed to take action to address. And they were arguing constantly, especially when they drank a couple of bottles of wine, which they did frequently. Transiting Mars went retrograde in Aries for several months, near natal Saturn at the 2nd house cusp, and opposite Moon and Mars in the 8th house. This was a contentious time when some large credit card debts accumulated

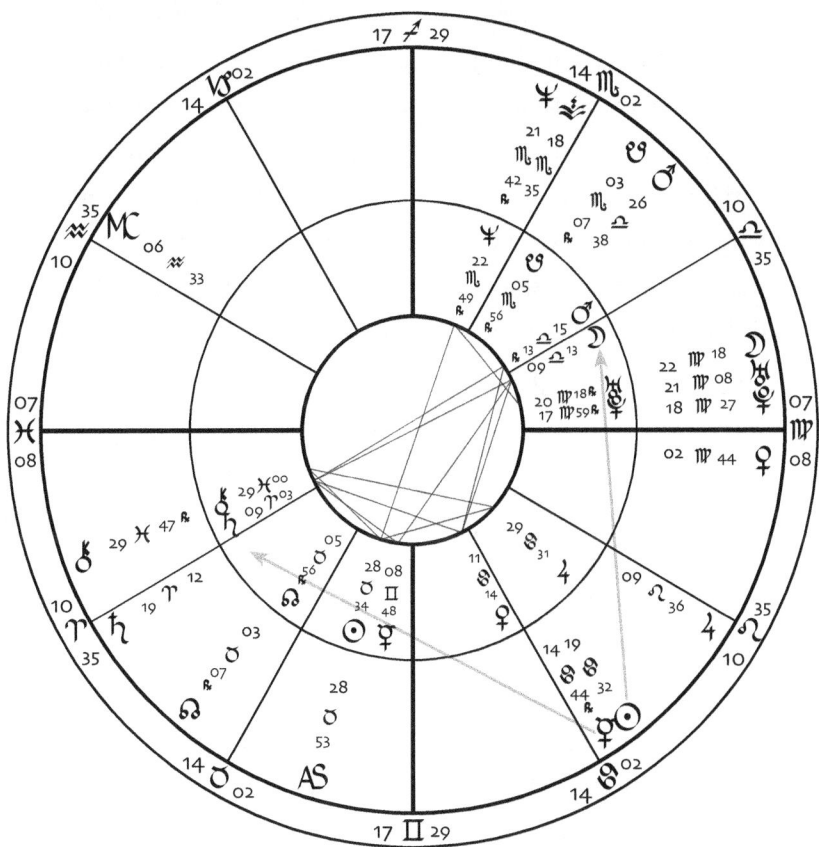

Louis – Inner wheel natal chart/outer wheel Naibod Secondary September 10, 2020

and everyone was getting a little snippy. They considered breaking up. The progressed moon in Virgo was in Louis's 7th house, and they were both expressing dissatisfaction with each other, and Randall suffered from severe digestive problems (progressed Moon in 7th house, conjunct Uranus and Pluto in Virgo). He'd undergone extensive diagnostic testing, which was so far inconclusive. I asked an innocent question, whether the digestive problems might be related to their intake of wine. Louis had Randall ask his physician about this. He reported back to me that they both decided to take a break from drinking for a while, changing their lifestyle (Virgo); they did it together (7th house) and within a few weeks Randall was starting to feel better. Then, prepped about the upcoming Jupiter-Saturn conjunction in December 2020, which would oppose Louis's natal Jupiter, ruler of his 10th house, making this a possibly auspicious moment, Louis carried out a plan to return to the company headquarters and he successfully pitched a bold product line and marketing strategy and was in the process of being rehired as a part-time consultant. Contemplating transiting Jupiter and Saturn entering his 12th house in Aquarius, I told Louis, "My vision for you is that you launch a fashion line that blazes a fresh trail in the industry, you sell this idea, then you step back into the background (12th house), let other people execute the plan, and you collect residuals in perpetuity." He laughed and said, "That's precisely what I plan to do, that's the exact course of action I'm pursuing." As transiting Uranus turned stationary direct conjunct his natal north node in Taurus, money started to flow again, right when he really needed it.

Zina

When I first looked at the chart of a client named Zina, I noted her Moon conjunct the MC, squaring her Cancer Sun, and opposite Jupiter and Saturn in the 4th house. The prominent placement of the Moon prompted me to I ask if she was a mother, and she answered affirmatively. I described how the chart showed a strong emphasis on family, home, domestic life,

Astrological Relationship Counseling: Nine Vignettes

and nurturing and support of family members. In the first five minutes of our session she told me that she has been a single mother for ten years and now lives with her two children and her mother (Moon at the MC). It turns out Zina's mother is a dominant figure, highly assertive, who owns the house the family lives in. I took a quick glance at the ephemeris and noted that ten years ago, in 2011–2012, transiting Pluto crossed her Descendant. I asked if her husband had suddenly changed, becoming hostile, explosive, contemptuous, controlling, toxic, resentful, and exuding negativity. Zina said, "All of the above. That describes him exactly."

I said, "It might have felt like you no longer recognized the man you were married to, like he'd been taken into the underworld." I continued, "I

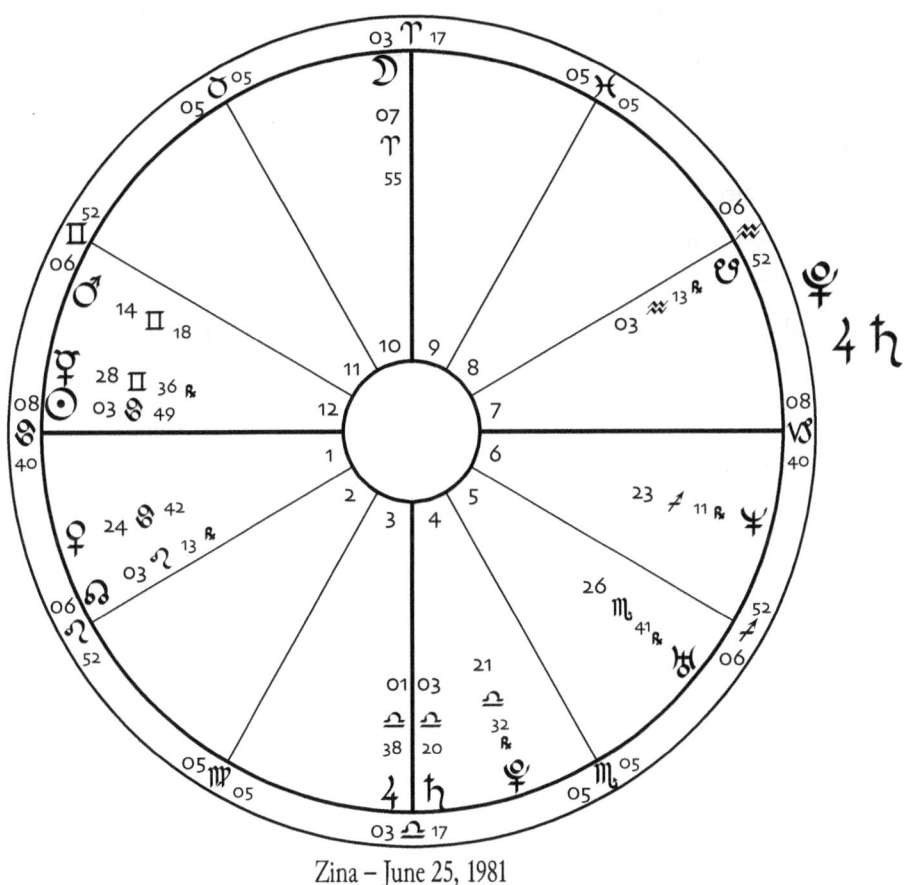

Zina – June 25, 1981

think you were committed to the marriage, with Jupiter-Saturn in Libra, the sign of marriage, but you couldn't take it anymore." I thought this situation might be especially difficult for her because, I noted, she had natal Pluto in her 4th house, and I wondered if she'd experienced any family turmoil or domestic violence in her family of origin. That question was evocative and Zina said, "Dad was physically abusive to my mother and my brother, which caused my mother to ultimately divorce him." "So mother was an excellent role model in that sense of not tolerating volcanic, violent behavior, but for the past ten years you must have been resonating with the bad feelings from the end of that relationship. Now your karma with that man is over; it is finished." I asked her if she was seeing anybody now, and noted that more recently, in 2018–2019, Saturn had entered her 7th house, and was now entering the 8th house along with Jupiter. She said that yes, she was seeing a man named Wendell. I described how appropriate it was that in 2020 there was a triple conjunction of Jupiter-Saturn, and Pluto in her 7th house, and during that year she and Wendell were becoming closer and more committed to each other. I said that Saturn in the 7th house is a crucial and important time for finding and building a relationship and possibly defining it. Now they were entering a phase of deeper intimacy and commitment (8th house). She said "He wants me to work on my money issues before he'll move in with me, but we're moving in that direction." Zina seemed to glow at that moment and I was struck by the power of Pluto to catalyze endings and elimination of toxic influences, clearing space for new beginnings.

The stories in this chapter illustrate a number of ways astrology can enhance our experience of relationships. Astrological insights can increase self-awareness of disagreeable behavior patterns such as destructive anger (Wayne); aid in maturation as a parent by letting go of responsibility for a child who has reached adulthood, and give hope for renewed cycles of social vitality after periods of bereavement (Tina); facilitate reconciliation of estranged family members, and shed light on ancestral, intergenerational influences affecting family relationships and the individual psyche, emerging from the horoscope's 4th house (Alice); indicate the appropriateness of a decisive breakup after incidents of marital infidelity (Amy); illuminate the tests of love and devotion that emerge in caring for a loved one, facing the end of life, and helping a partner die (Mary); teach patience and tolerance, compassionate understanding of a spouse's occupational stresses, and acceptance of unconventional family roles defying traditional gender stereotypes (Allen and Cathy); help a person recover self-respect after a divorce, and validate relationships focused on spiritual or intellectual pursuits rather than romance and eros (Ellen); indicate the importance of lifestyle changes and responsibly facing financial and medical challenges together (Louis); and shed light on changing cycles and phases of love such as the ending of one relationship and the commencement of another one (Zina).

Chapter 3

Astrotherapeutic Interventions

In this chapter I'll discuss two in-depth examples of therapeutic astrological work. Both stories involve the Saturn return and both illustrate the use of astrology in the treatment of substance abuse. These examples illustrate the interplay between contrasting, polarized astrological energies that manifested in both internal and external conflicts. The first example also refers to the practice of combining astrology with dream interpretation, a topic I discussed at length in *Astrology's Higher Octaves*.

Jorge

Jorge had natal Mars conjunct Uranus, Neptune, and Saturn. Working in the hi-tech industry, approaching his 30th birthday, he experienced marital problems due to his fixation on viewing pornography, his addiction to video gaming, alcohol abuse, and excessive pot smoking. His wife threatened to leave him, and he was written up at work for being late, for disinterest and not completing assignments, for numerous outbursts, twice yelling at his boss, and he was put on probation, and forced to take a leave of absence to pursue therapy.

With this conjunction involving Neptune in his 4th house, there was multi-generational alcoholism in Jorge's family, which he detailed for me. Now he was drinking alone and isolating from his wife. Note the natal conjunction of Mars-Uranus, symbolizing an urge for freedom, rebellion and unconstrained sexual drives, and also the belligerent, defiant, obstinate attitude that can get a man within an inch of being fired from a secure

Astrology as a Therapeutic Art

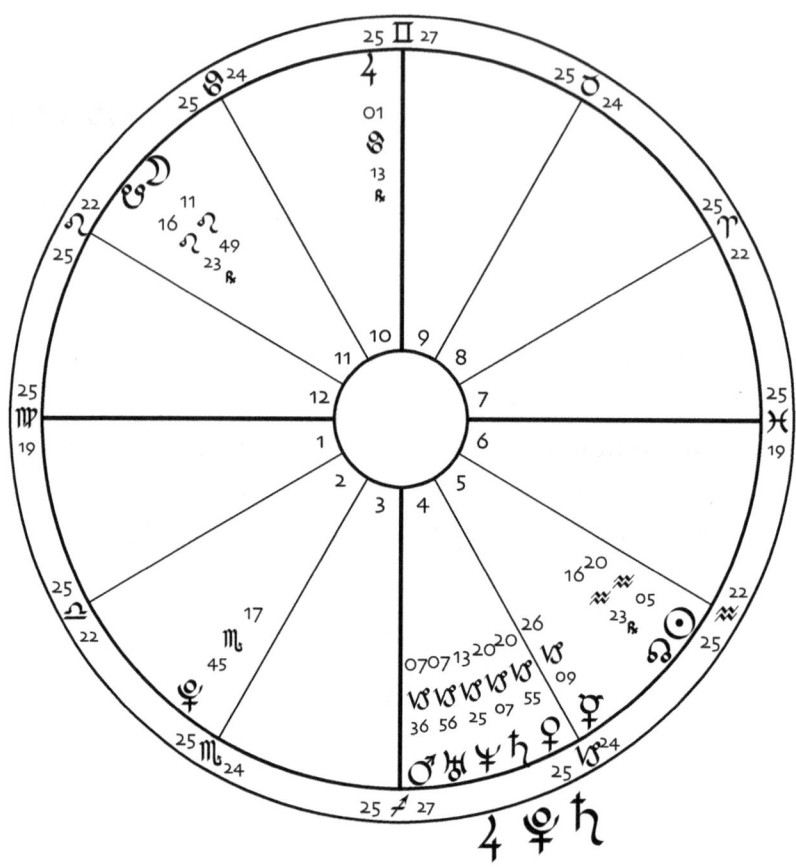

Jorge – February 8, 1990

job. His Mars-Neptune conjunction found him constantly in a haze, procrastinating on several fronts, and magnifying the problem, Neptune, planet of drug and alcohol abuse, was conjunct both Uranus and Saturn. He was experiencing his Saturn return, a transit that often involves an urge for maturity, sobriety, and self-control. Jorge told me this dream:

> I am on a roller coaster that ended right before hitting the water. I'm trying to save the people on the roller coaster, trying to make it stop. Then I see Daniel Cormier, a champion UFC fighter, one of my role models, a really good guy. He's my father figure in the dream.

44

We were in a car going to an event. This was a once in a lifetime opportunity to spend time with him.

The roller coaster reminded Jorge of highs and lows, twists and turns, high speed emotional ups and downs. "When I drink I get angry and emotional. I drink so I don't have to think about my emotions." I said, "You and your wife are on a roller coaster, with lots of arguing. I think the dream is saying that you need to rescue yourself, stop the roller coaster before it hits the water, before it crashes, before your marriage crashes. Now tell me about this person you're in the car with that you say is your role model and a really good guy." Jorge said, "Before he was UFC champion, Daniel was an Olympic gold medalist as a wrestler; he helps children in cities. He's a stand up guy. He's clean and doesn't do steroids. I said, "The Daniel part of you is emerging at this time when transiting Saturn is returning to its natal position—the Saturn return. You have an opportunity to drive in the car with him and to become closer to this admired figure."

Jorge said that Daniel's main rival in the Ultimate Fighting Championship is Jon Jones, whom he described as "a scoundrel who once crashed a car and left the scene—totally unacceptable. He's out of control, has stints with the law. He takes banned steroids. He's a horrible human being." I said, "The Jon Jones part of you is a rebel who tries to get away with doing things that your wife doesn't like and forbids you to do; Jones skirts the rules. That rebellious side of you relates to your Mars-Uranus conjunction. Daniel is an Olympic champion who presumably got there through hard work, training, and self-discipline. He represents the emergence of Saturn in your consciousness. His presence here suggests to me that, with the right focus, the high energy of your Mars-Uranus can become laser sharp in pursuit of your goals. The fact that you're in the car with a gold medalist in the dream symbolizes your potential. Daniel represents being good, virtuous, sober, law abiding, and healthy. Jon Jones represents being sneaky, law abusing, a villain, engaging in misconduct, feeling like you can break the rules and get away with it. [Think of Mars conjunct Uranus.] He's an image of your shadow, and represents a part of you that can be self-undermining, which relates to Neptune conjunct Saturn." He replied, "When I drink and get wasted I feel like a horrible human being." I said, "It will take a heroic act of courage to change your patterns of substance abuse and to overcome the deeply rooted family illness of alcoholism, which emerged out of their experiences of suffering and adversity in Mexico, signified in your chart by the 4th house planets, where we often see intergenerational influences." The polarity between these two subpersonalities embodied the tensions implied by natal Saturn conjunct Uranus and Neptune. These insights became the basis for some intensive therapy as Jorge began to form a path and lifestyle of recovery. After some time, he was able to return to work, and that was the last I heard from him.

Optimizing Our Adaptation to Stress

At each stage of life we're faced with various stressors, which are inevitable. Jorge had transiting Saturn conjunct Mars in his 4th house, showing stressors in the extended family, and an inflamed situation in his household. Harvard professor George Vaillant's Theory of Mature Adaptation describes a continuum of responses to the stresses of life, which he says range from adaptive to maladaptive, which means they're self-defeating and interfere with our development.

- *Psychotic adaptations*: paranoia, hallucination.

- *Immature adaptations*: acting out, passive aggressive behavior, hypochondria, projection, idle fantasy, refusing help and not seeking help, not taking action. Major image distortion: learned helplessness.

- *Neurotic adaptations* (used by most people): intellectualization, rationalization, denial, repression (refusing to acknowledge that something is happening, or has happened); dissociation (removal

Astrotherapeutic Interventions

from one's feelings); memory lapses. Minor image distortion: unrealistic, overly inflated or deflated self-image.

- *Mature adaptations*: altruism, humor, anticipation, planning, suppression (a conscious decision to postpone action); sublimation: finding healthy outlets for expressing feelings. Moderation. Maturity is aligned with making choices and consciously directly our behaviors.

On the low end of the continuum of coping behaviors there are *psychotic adaptations:* paranoia and hallucination. Years ago I knew a woman with an exact Sun-Neptune opposition, right across her Ascendant and Descendant, and she was one of the most inspiring, mystical people I've ever known. But she was also delusional and couldn't function in society or consensus reality; she spoke her own language that other people couldn't follow, and years later she became convinced that she was a star person from an advanced galaxy come to earth to start a celestial mystery school to take humanity to the next level. Her deluded, inflationary thinking was quite off-putting to other people, who increasingly avoided her.

Next, there are *immature adaptations:* hypochondria, projection, idle fantasy, inaction, refusing help and not seeking help; also *major image distortion*, or learned helplessness. I have seen a number of clients who felt they were unable to stop looking at porn or video games, sometimes to the point of divorce and job loss. Astrologically, many of these immature responses to stress are linked to the influence of Neptune. We saw this with Jorge. This was an individual who also exhibited a number of *neurotic adaptations*, including rationalization, denial, repression (refusing to acknowledge that something is happening, or has happened); avoidant behavior; dissociation (removal from one's feelings); and memory lapses. There's also *minor image distortion*, evident in an unrealistic, overly inflated or deflated self-image. Jorge told me, "I used to think 'They'll never fire me.' I thought I was irreplaceable. Then I was nearly canned."

According to Five Factor Theory, neurotic traits include debilitating anxiety, angry hostility, major depression, impulsivity, addiction, extreme self-consciousness (being painfully shy), and an extreme need for control. These are self-defeating personality traits that interfere with successful adaptation to life. I once had as a client a physician with Sun square Neptune who was addicted to numerous prescription drugs, pills for his heart, his blood pressure, pain meds, anti-anxiety drugs, antidepressants, and sleep medications. For years he never confided in anybody about this, never sought help. I said to him, "You're the medical expert here. But don't you think it is possible you're getting a lot of unintended interactive effects between all of these medications. I'm concerned that might not be good for you. Your dependence on all these medications is maladaptive, not an optimal way to cope with the stress of your medical career and marriage." It was a huge step when he was able to accept help and treatment from another physician, and he successfully went through supervised detox in a hospital.

Alcoholism and addictions are some of the most common neurotic responses to stressors. Personally, I think there's a place in life for responsible enjoyment of alcohol and cannabis, but it is problematic when overindulgence causes impairments of our health, our job performance, our driving skills, or our ability to show up for our loved ones.

Bailee

This is the chart of Bailee, who was a precociously successful executive approaching her first Saturn return. In her mid twenties Bailee rose swiftly through the corporate ranks as a Human Resources manager overseeing many employees. Her chart features a conjunction of Saturn, Uranus, and Neptune in Capricorn in the 6th house of employment, benefits, and workplace dynamics. The preponderance in Capricorn signifies her abilities in business administration and handling large responsibilities. Her career advancement was timed by transiting Pluto in Capricorn conjunct her natal Capricorn planets and Uranus in Aries squaring those planets. She expressed satisfaction at the independence her job afforded her to work from home, with flexible hours. She was making good money. That was all working well. But there were two big problem areas in her life, and they were inter-related. Her relationships were not working out. She had harsh breakups with several girlfriends, and the biggest destabilizing factor was her propensity to binge drinking. She would hold it together for a while, with Saturn creating a controlled, buttoned-up executive persona, but barely able to hold in check the unruly energies of Uranus and Neptune, which combined to keep her chasing a state of ecstasy, losing all self-control when she went out to bars, and she quickly became unspooled as she'd become belligerent and start fights that sometimes got physical, unleashing the fire of her Sun-Mars conjunction. Then she felt horrible about herself and went into long depressive moods—one of the ways Saturn-Neptune aspects sometimes manifest.

Bailee was in the grips of a repeating pattern. It was like she became possessed by another personality. The Saturn persona was well polished, demur, and appropriate. Her shadow was sarcastic, caustic, mistrustful, attacking, and deeply wounded. I interpret the natal Moon-Mars conjunction as a symbol of what John Bowlby termed *insecure-ambivalent attachment*, which is characterized by mistrustfulness, with cycles of desperate clinging to an attachment figure followed by attack and punishment of that person. Arguably she exhibited some of the traits of borderline personality, with a history of volatile, unstable relationships, depression, a tendency toward substance abuse (for Bailee it was mixing booze with pot and MDMA), and periods of decompensation (disorganization, falling apart), all linked to an underlying fear of abandonment and rage at the disappointing object or person who can never fully reassure them or meet their needs.

After each breakup Bailee got more depressed and down on herself, and every time she drank she felt horrible, physically and emotionally. With Sun and Moon in Virgo and Saturn in the 6th house, she cared a lot about her job and workplace. Sometimes she'd feel discouraged after difficult staff meetings or rounds of employee layoffs or intimations that the company was about to be sold, and that would set off a drinking spree. During this time she dated a few women she described as mean drunks, and several times she felt victimized and physically and verbally abused; relational victimization is a major contributor to depression and is linked to Neptune. And sometimes her own aggression, shown in the natal Sun-Mars conjunction, was unleashed. In our initial sessions I tried to feel and understand the inner turmoil she was experiencing.

A key event occurred in 2018 when solar arc Mars came into conjunction with her natal Venus and Bailee met Karin, her soulmate. Some months

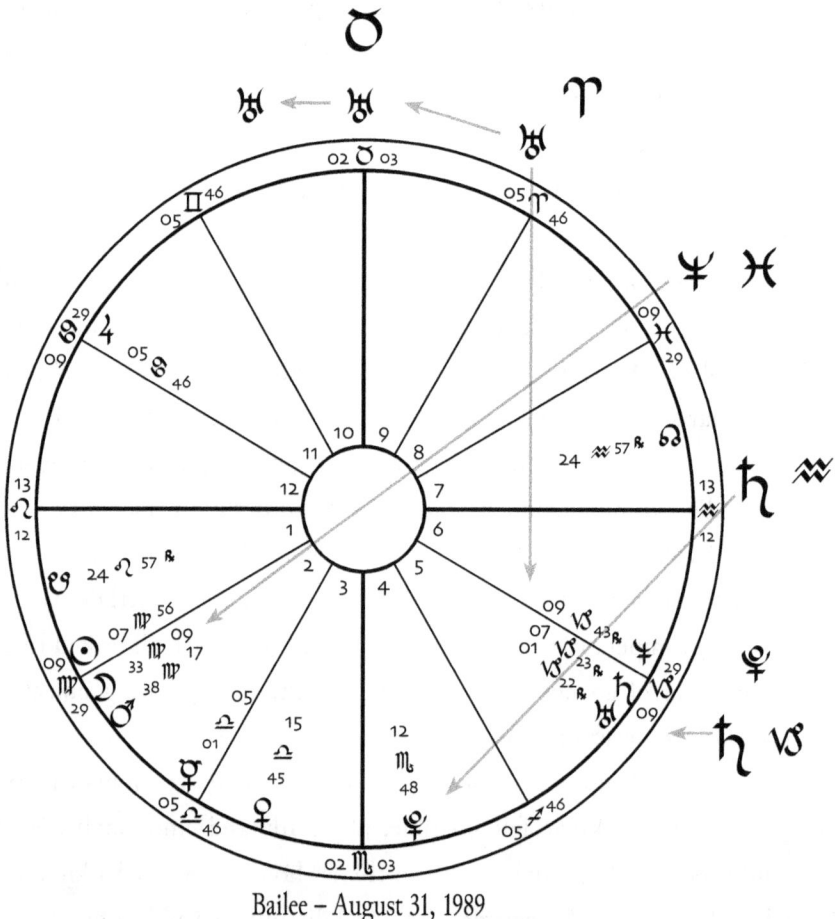

Bailee – August 31, 1989

later in early 2019 she also had a progressed New Moon in Libra (March 2019), and it seemed that they had a chance to really form a relationship and become a couple, but it was a rocky road at first. Soon after she took Karin home to meet her parents for the first time, the two of them got drunk and started a fight that spun out of control. Then Bailee was in a complete meltdown with suicidal thoughts. This occurred the evening of a Moon-Mars-Neptune conjunction in Pisces, apt symbolism for a night of drinking and loss of perspective: Note how the transiting Moon-Mars repeats her natal conjunction, triggering impulsive expression of anger. She feared she may have ruined her new relationship, regretted her actions and her words, and started trying to get sober. She admitted, "I become unhinged with alcohol." She was also taking Xanax and Adderoll and it is contraindicated to mix these medications with hard alcohol.

As Uranus passed over her MC Bailee had several more drinking binges—too many, she said. And she felt an inner urge to change. During her Saturn return she began regularly attending AA meetings where she enjoyed the reliable structure and format, the feeling of being with people who cared, and felt the support for her abstinence and sobriety. It is adaptive stress coping to seek help and support when we need it, and the AA meetings definitely helped her stop drinking for a while. This was a positive evolution of Saturn conjunct Neptune.

She realized she was such a better version of herself when she didn't consume alcohol. It was much easier to maintain self-control in her actions and demeanor, and this allowed her to form a loving and trusting relationship with Karin. She was simply more agreeable. In Five Factor Theory, *agreeableness* describes traits that enhance relationships and make positive outcomes more likely, such as modesty, trust, trustworthiness, compliance, and straightforwardness. People have less favorable relational outcomes when they're disagreeable, conceited, devious, suspicious, uncooperative, unyielding, and untrustworthy. With her natal Venus in Libra, Bailee was capable of being a congenial partner, and this was something she wanted to strive for.

Five Factor Personality Theory can be summarized by the acronym OCEAN:

> *Openness:* open-mindedness, openness to experience; flexibility; openness of ideas and feelings; imagination, intuition; considers alternatives. Opposite of rigidity, closed-mindedness. Gullibility, innocence.
>
> *Conscientiousness:* competence, order, dutifulness, achievement striving, self-discipline, deliberation. Opposite of carelessness, sloppiness.
>
> *Extraversion:* Warmth, gregariousness, assertiveness, activity, excitement-seeking, positive emotions, enthusiasm.
>
> *Agreeableness:* Trust (opposite of suspicion or paranoia), straightforwardness, trustworthiness, altruism, compliance, modesty. Can be "too nice," overly compliant.
>
> *Neuroticism:* anxiety, angry hostility, depression, addiction, self-consciousness, impulsivity, vulnerability; extreme need for control.

The couple got in another fight while on vacation in Mexico, and some sharp claws came out. Bailee began to recognize that, with her Sun-Moon-Mars in Virgo, she was exacting, sharp, excoriating, and capable of withering criticism of her partner. She was also tense and anxious about Karin's health, as she had several conditions and Bailee was anxious to get more information about that. I asked her to search inwardly to understand her extreme anxiety about this, and she recalled that during her childhood, her mother had various health complaints and was preoccupied and not consistently available, so Bailee developed mistrustfulness, an expectation of being disappointed, and a lot of anger about unmet needs (Moon conjunct Mars).

Astrotherapeutic Interventions

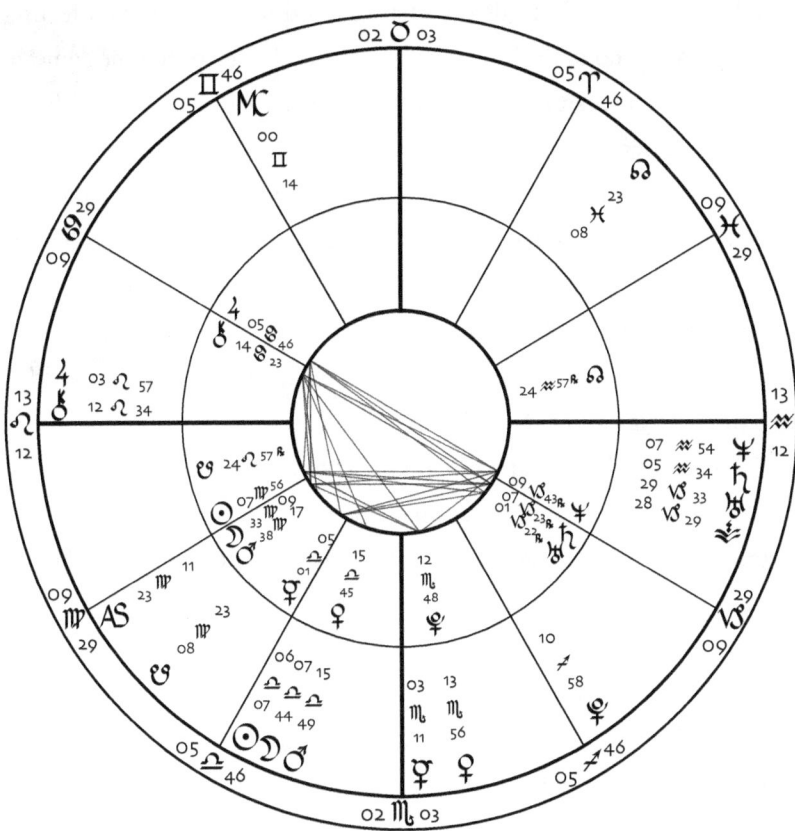

Bailee – Inner wheel natal chart/outer wheel Solar Arc Direction August 1, 2018

With transiting Uranus at her MC she had several new job offers to consider, so her career was still in motion. And this, coupled with the recent emotional roller coaster, was somewhat dizzying for her. I recall one day saying "With Saturn conjunct natal Saturn and Neptune in the 6th house of health and self-improvement, I think you need your Saturn to gain mastery and self-control over your habits; for you, drinking is a disease. It disorganizes you, and unleashes an angry bully that's angry and dissatisfied with everything and full of resentment. It disturbs your health and your ability to do your job. Alcohol is a depressant and wreaks havoc when you combine it with medications you take. I think you need to develop a different kind of spiritual life and learn to access a feeling of expansiveness without alcohol." This prompted Bailee to tell me something about the hidden history of her family. Apparently her grandfather was murdered and her grandmother was somehow involved. It was a very creepy story that seemed linked to Pluto in her 4th house, which is sometimes a symbol of intergenerational family trauma. For years her father had been investigating, trying to get to the bottom of this event, which happened when he was 7 years old. She said, "When Dad and his new wife recently came to visit us they were drinking all day during their visit, just like he drank when I was a kid. Now I remember where my own behavior comes from." These comments put a fine point on our understanding of Neptune, planet of alcoholism, conjunct Saturn, the father.

I told her, "During the Saturn return, structures get set in place that become enduring. In your case, natal Saturn is conjunct Neptune. The way I see it, by the end of your Saturn return you either get this under your control and you'll be in recovery, or you'll be set in the patterns and habits of an alcoholic. It's up to you which path you choose." In that moment Bailee and I reached a level of truth and emotional honesty that had a tangible resonance.

In his book *The Art of the Psychotherapist,* James Bugental[7] describes how a therapist guides clients in sessions that advance through several conversational levels, starting with formalities when counselor and client are first introduced and seek to make a good impression on the other. *Contact maintenance* begins with transitional conversation and small talk with little self-disclosure, and transitions to *standard conversation* focused on collecting factual information, taking a history, for example, an educational or vocational history, or the history of marriages, names of family members, previous therapy or experiences with other astrologers. Standard conversation then gives way to an invitation to change level, which occurs during *critical occasions,* where clients make themselves truly accessible to the impact of therapeutic dialogue. Here clients express their authentic inner experiencing and the therapist genuinely meets them in this depth. Critical occasions are conversations that make a difference. These turning points in counseling occur when the therapist gets real with their perception of a person and their assessment of a problem. Here the therapist goes beyond listening, guiding, instructing, or rational advising and is willing to risk honesty and expressing their own feelings, values, and convictions in order to persuade, to exercise "interpersonal press." These critical occasions are conversations that result in genuine changes, crossroads talks from which we emerge with a change in perspective, attitude, or emotion.[8]

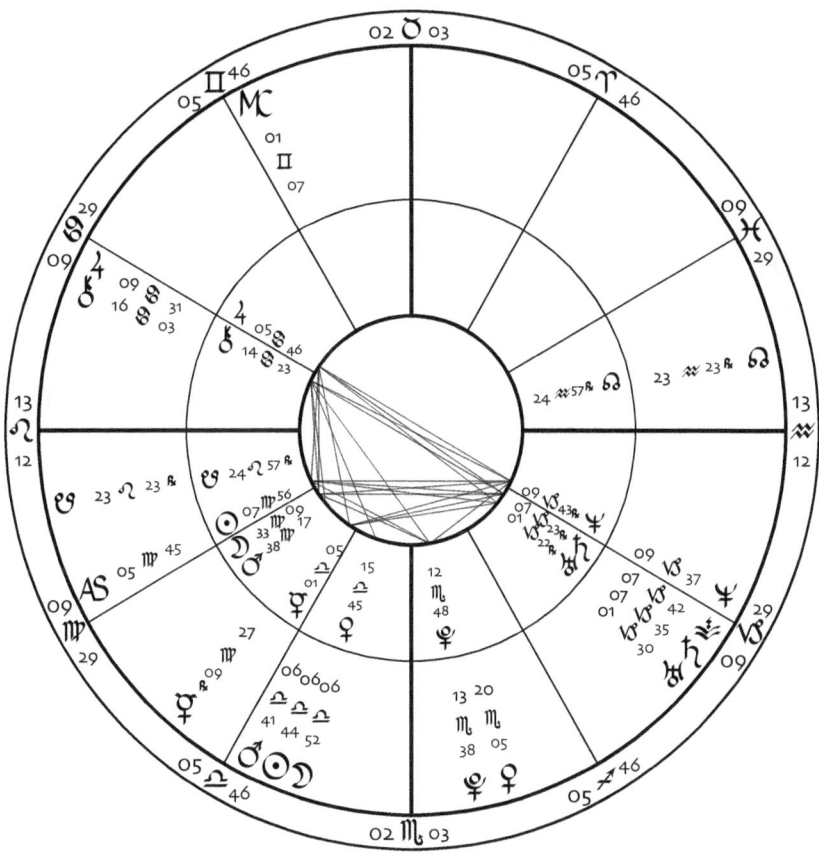

Bailee – Inner wheel natal chart/outer wheel Naibod Secondary March 15, 2019

Astrology as a Therapeutic Art

I talked to Bailee a few years later, in February of 2022. I learned that when transiting Saturn in Aquarius entered her 7th house and squared her natal Pluto in her 4th house she and Karin bought a home, an older house, and they were doing renovations, which was a nice outlet for her Moon-Sun-Mars conjunction in Virgo. She enjoyed doing physical work and was learning some new carpentry skills. Recently, in 2020, her progressed Sun was square Saturn and progressed Saturn; she'd settled down into a position with a stable employer. She and Karin got married. Also, the 2020 Jupiter-Saturn conjunction occurred in her 6th house. She got promoted to a higher level of corporate management. Her health habits had improved considerably. She hadn't had a drink for two years. I wondered about her progressed Sun

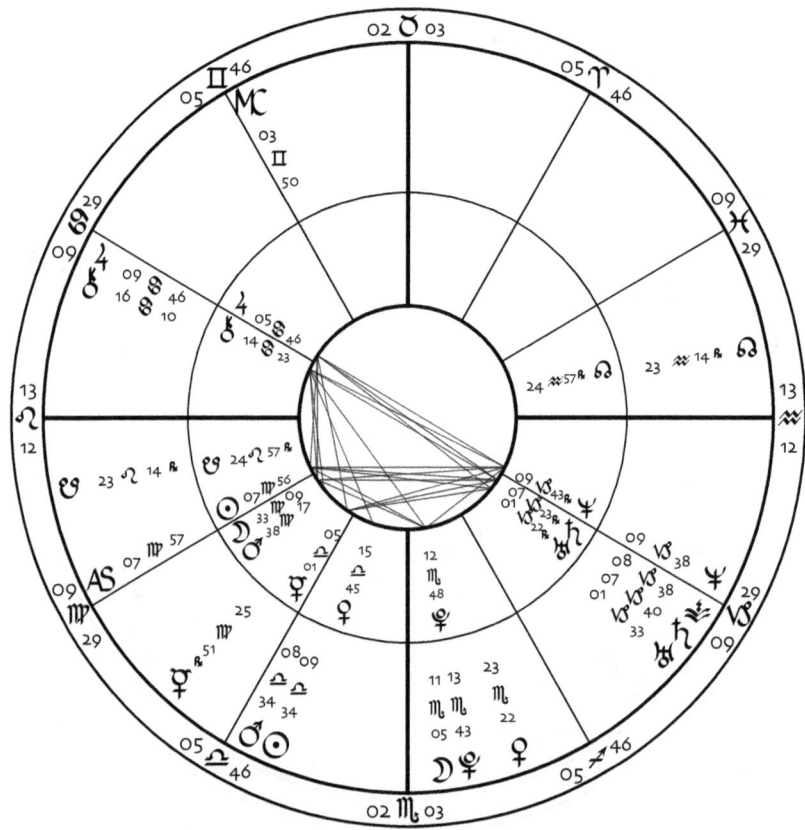

Bailee – Inner wheel natal chart/outer wheel Nailbod Secondary February 3, 2022

square natal Neptune, but she said, "I drink tons of water. The only thing I do is smoke some weed." She was running and lifting weights and enjoying protein shakes.

I noted that, in addition to transiting Saturn square Pluto, she was currently in the midst of a progressed Moon-Pluto conjunction in Scorpio in her 4th house, which I thought could indicate some emotional crisis, catharsis, or eruption related to family issues. Bailee recounted how over the holidays she got in a fight with her mother, frustrated with feeling responsible for her. "I have to be the parent around my mom. I can't relax around her." I said, "With natal Moon conjunct Mars in Virgo, you feel anxious around your mother. And I imagine that sometimes you're very critical of her."

She replied, "Mother is smothering, suffocating. I feel like I always have to take care of her. But now I see how Mom has been displaced by the divorce; she is exiled, and feels very alone." I replied, "Your parents' divorce is still powerfully resonating during this Moon-Pluto conjunction in Scorpio in the family 4th house." She said, "Dad was drinking and having an affair. Mom is the aggrieved party. She was wronged and abandoned." I said, "It's interesting how the downward spiral of their marriage was directly linked to alcohol abuse." And she said, "I'd never made the connection between that and the trauma my dad experienced."

Bailee was focusing on health, exercise, diet, and excellence at work. Also, she had progressed Sun-Saturn square: she is two years sober. By any measure, she has found more mature, fulfilling forms of adaptation to life, and has worked to develop and refine her personality. In the terms of Five Factor Theory, she was high in conscientiousness as a strong, disciplined professional. Her agreeableness was enhanced by sobriety. She had worked to minimize the expression of angry hostility. And according to Vaillant, a high adaptive form of stress coping is altruism, trying to help others. Bailee got involved as an AA sponsor and volunteered a few hours a month at an animal shelter.

Chapter 4

Relationships in Transition: Pathways of Change

The wisdom of astrology—revealed through intuition, through consistent application of the core techniques of transits and progressions, and through spontaneous process work in sessions or at home writing in my journals—informs how I relate to people in my life and also guides my professional practice as a marriage and family therapist, where my occupational mission is to protect, preserve, and heal human relationships. As astrologers studying our natal charts we come to define our identities and envision the shape of who and what we're supposed to be, and we also seek to understand the identity of others and how to co-exist with them, meeting the tests of interaction through different time phases—indicated by planetary influences such as transits and progressions affecting the 7th house, its dispositor, and its various derived houses.

Certain planetary alignments shed light on periods when people aren't getting along with each other, and also give us the opportunity to look at how our own actions or behaviors are contributing to discord. For example, under the influence of Neptune we might avoid confrontation or numb our feelings with too much alcohol or vegetative TV viewing; with Uranus it could be a disruptive pattern of distancing or pushing another person away; with Mars it might be impulsivity or a tendency to bristle with anger too readily—running too hot. Our planetary science gives abundant clues that clarify what we might do to improve our interpersonal relations.

Astrology as a Therapeutic Art

This chapter is another gallery of stories of people who bravely worked through various relational challenges. These stories remind us of situations we've encountered or are facing now, or someone we know is going through it, and they show the power of astrology to help us become better and more fulfilled human beings. In the next example, I look at a small number of chart symbols and their meaning in microscopic detail over a series of sessions, to explore the nuances of a relationship. Here I focus almost entirely on the Moon, as Moon's natal placement and aspects signify our core complexes—recurring, emotionally charged issues and unconscious patterns of behavior that often become sore spots and create stress in our social interactions.

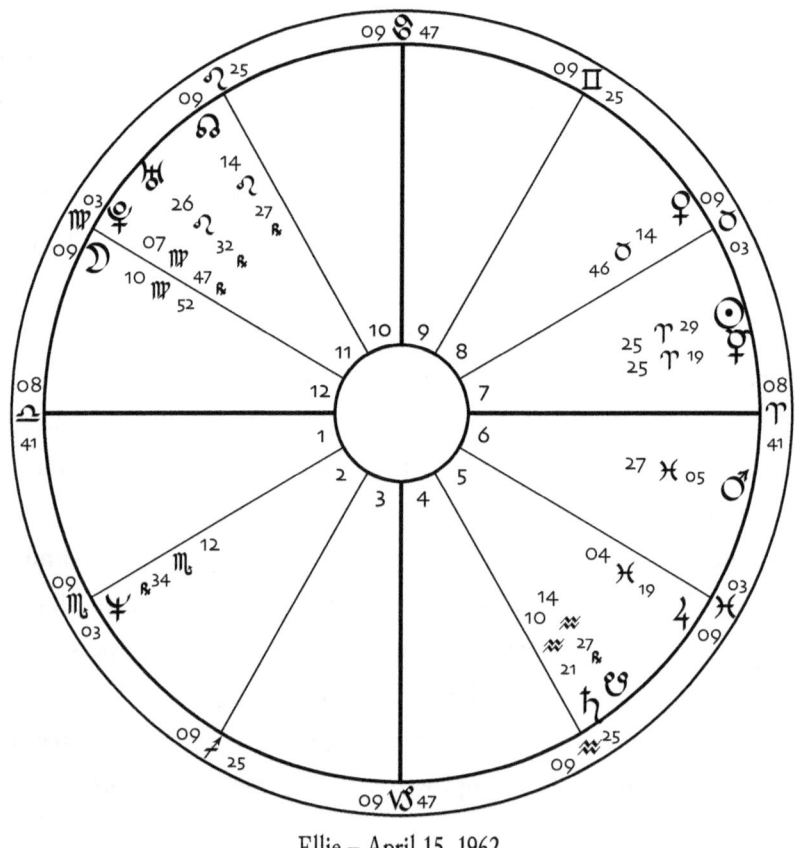

Ellie – April 15, 1962

Ellie and Bret

I recall a couple I worked with years ago, Ellie and Bret. Ellie had a Moon-Pluto conjunction in Virgo in the 12th house. At first I asked a rather broad question, whether she had any problems or stress related to her mother. She described her mother as critical and full of resentment and negativity, and then said that she herself is obsessive, perfectionistic, and highly critical of her husband. I learned that she was emotionally volatile, was frequently resentful while cooking, which lessened both of their enjoyment in sitting down and eating meals together; and when Bret asked for hugs or a little contact she felt controlled, like his needs were engulfing and suffocating, so she recoiled from him. Sex had been out of the question for quite some time. With her Sun-Mercury conjunction in Aries, she felt Bret was always asking, demanding, pleading. In her eyes, he was very selfish and all about himself. That is how she perceived him. And her own ram's horns rose up and the two of them were constantly locking horns. Aries isn't a sign known foremost for being agreeable, cooperative, and pleasant. With Aries Sun in the 7th house, Ellie described Bret as abrupt and disagreeable, but he quickly replied that she was equally unpleasant and that she seemed angry and shut down most of the time. They were sniping at each other in real time in our session.

Ellie and Bret were a classic "approach–avoid couple," with one person seeking more closeness and the other needing more distance and space. Both of them were suffering in different ways, Ellie because Bret wasn't good enough and seemed to do everything wrong, which was how her mother always made her feel; and Bret because Ellie was emotionally and physically distant and decidedly ungratifying. I no longer have Bret's natal chart but I recall that he had a Moon-Neptune conjunction in Scorpio at the Midheaven and that he longed for soothing, comforting, and the safe harbor of his wife's embrace. Bret felt confused and unsettled by Ellie's rejection of his pleading for connection and reassurance of her love. Both parties were affected by past conditioning, and through our astrological work we tried to shed light on that conditioning by having them learn about each other's charts.

I said, "Ellie, with your 7th house Sun I think on some level you want your mate and your relationship to become the center of your world and the locus of your identity as a partner. But your 12th house Moon-Pluto seems to withdraw into a shell like a turtle, pulling inward. Once Bret does something that irks you, you step back and refuse to connect."

Bret acknowledged to Ellie that his messiness around the home was a flash point and a major cause of her dissatisfaction. In her eyes, he was oblivious to the chaos he created around him (Moon-Neptune). He understood that it would make her Virgo Moon happy if he'd make a few simple behavioral changes, picking up his clothes and putting them away, washing the dishes but also the pots and pans, and the countertops, and the stove burners. And taking out the garbage. Keeping things clean, being thorough—that would be greatly appreciated, if he'd just try to adopt her Virgo Moon's way of life. He grasped what it would mean if he were to act as if Ellie's chart were his own. When we commit to a relationship it's as if we acquire a second chart that we can work with and make a part of us. This is related to John Gottman's insight that in healthy couples partners allow themselves to be influenced by each other.[9] When we introduce astrology into the process of understanding a relationship we continue to inhabit our own identities shown in the birth chart, but we also consciously adapt to the other person's chart and their way of being and try to harmonize with it. We weave some completely new cloth out of a shared interactive space where our respective natal patterns and energies deliberately interact. The process begins by getting the individuals to understand each other's charts and their behavior and motivations. This starts conversations that quickly build an emotional charge and bring key issues into focus.

Discussing the aggressive qualities of Scorpio Moon conjunct Neptune, Ellie said that Bret's complaining often devolved into biting attacks and accusations, emotional overreactions based on misperceptions and projections, and persecutory fantasies that Ellie wanted to hurt him and enjoyed toying with him. She was always promising closeness and then finding a reason to get furious and storm off in a black cloud, so he felt manipulated. Ellie described how Bret punished her relentlessly with his passive-aggressive behavior around the house, which infuriated her, and his slovenly appearance in public, which on several occasions had caused her some embarrassment—very distressing for her proper Virgo Moon. Moreover, she felt his physical approach to her was rough, engulfing, and emotionally insatiable. It was like he had no boundaries and repeatedly tried to grope her. All of this was somewhat difficult and embarrassing for the two of them to discuss, but they were revealing part of their lived experience as a couple. These were feelings and perceptions of each other that needed to be aired.

Bret agreed that Ellie's sense of him as needy and demanding were not invalid. He did crave more nourishing physical connection with her. We allowed space in the session for Bret to express that this was something he needed if the relationship was going to work for him. Sex was a basic need for his Scorpio Moon. He said he was sensitive to Ellie's rejection because his alcoholic mother had emotionally abandoned him and was unreliable, which shone a new light on the meaning of his Moon-Neptune. He also understood Ellie's feeling that his pleading for connection could be cloying and insipid. I ventured the interpretation that Moon-Neptune suggested an emotional and spiritual longing to be enfolded by a larger wholeness, to feel contact with a nourishing maternal ground and to experience a moment of biochemical and energetic union. I said, "Ultimately Bret, I think you want to feel that you're at one with the Mother of all existence." Bret turned to Ellie and said, "I feel that sense of union when we make love. I just want to experience that with you, and not fight about it." Ellie said she loved hearing that.

I said, "Ellie, I wonder what would happen if you'd try to adopt Bret's Moon-Neptune as your own, as a part of you, your own unconscious, and your potential. Can we try that? Take a moment to visualize and feel what it would be like to be the need-fulfilling mother who is devoted, attuned, and responsive to Bret, without resentment. And I know I'm suggesting something bold here, but I wonder if you can imagine and visualize that there is inside you a Scorpio Moon goddess who fulfills some of Bret's sexual fantasies and desires and actually enjoys it." Ellie said, "I know it makes Bret happy when I act like that goddess." The feeling in the room changed after that discussion as they realized they both wanted the same thing.

Later, we were discussing Ellie's Virgo Moon and her perfectionism and obsession with order. Bret expressed that he felt he could never relax around the house or leave a book or magazine or some financial paperwork on a coffee table. She didn't like the way he folded the laundry or made the bed, or the fact that she had to ask him to do these tasks. She disparaged his cooking. Lately it seemed that the smallest thing would send Ellie into a snit; she was always on patrol, watching for transgressions. That reminded Ellie of how her mother was constantly snooping on her. But at the same time there were other valid reasons for Ellie's anxious demeanor. Bret had been out of work for almost two months after getting laid off, and he didn't seem to be taking his job search seriously. With her Virgo Moon in the 12th house (the work–6th house from the husband–7th), it was important to her that her husband go to work. She said, "I've talked to you numerous times recently about your excessive beer drinking but my words fall on deaf ears. Honestly, I see you sloshed way too often." He replied, "It's my way of coping with being laid off. I worked for that company five years and they showed no loyalty to me whatsoever." This brought another level of meaning to Moon-Neptune at his Midheaven. Bret cared about that job and his career, and he felt abandoned and hurt and that all his hard work had been for nothing. He was experiencing loss, brooding depression, and desolation, and both Ellie and I expressed our compassion for how difficult that must be for him. But now, pointedly, Ellie's feedback in therapy was that alcohol abuse was blunting his ability to cope with the stresses in his life, stemming from unemployment and feeling unloved by his wife. It was maladaptive. It was sapping his confidence and motivation to pursue career opportunities and magnifying his sense of helplessness (Neptune).

Over a few weeks, Ellie tried to convince Bret to start attending AA meetings, but he said would handle the problem on his own and she confirmed that he had begun to dial back the beer guzzling and take a clearer look at his situation. Finally, in one of our sessions I said, "Bret, I invite you to take inside the feeling that Ellie deeply cares about you. Please take that in. I believe there is a reservoir of emotional supply available to you, if you become more secure in your attachment. I feel that your Moon-Neptune describes a longing for something of a mythical, archetypal nature—an idealized image of the all-good, gratifying mother. But no woman, no wife or mother, can fulfill or embody that ideal and that archetype all the time, so I think you can do a better job of managing your emotional disappointments and not becoming so mopey, moody, and depressed. The Moon-Neptune conjunction at your Midheaven suggests that you can discover this inner emotional reservoir through meditation and other spiritual practices that evoke an oceanic, expansive feeling, so you feel full and satisfied and less emotional craving and desperation and emptiness. A high expression of this Moon-Neptune would be to feel in your body that connection with the Mother source of all existence, so that you become serene and blissful." This was a moment where through the laser accuracy of astrological symbols, a man perceived in an instant a vision of his higher potential and who he could become.

Through this process work over a number of sessions Ellie and Bret came to understand themselves better, and they were able to sustain an enlivening marriage. They both became devotees of a spiritual teacher and practitioners of bhakti yoga, which further awakened the deep love and devotion symbolized by Ellie's Venus-Neptune opposition, squaring her nodal axis; and Bret became a strong meditator and uplifted his

Astrology as a Therapeutic Art

consciousness. Their story demonstrates how it's possible to build and renew relationships using astrological knowledge.

Trudy

Some people's birth charts indicate that the relational sphere is harmonious and relatively uncomplicated. For example, Trudy has Sun-Venus conjunction in her 7th house. She has been married for 44 years. Saturn in Libra in her 10th house suggests that achieving stability within the commitments of marriage was a primary evolutionary goal. With her Aries Moon in a T-square, square Uranus in Cancer and opposite Saturn, one might be concerned that relationships would be stressed. Over the years she

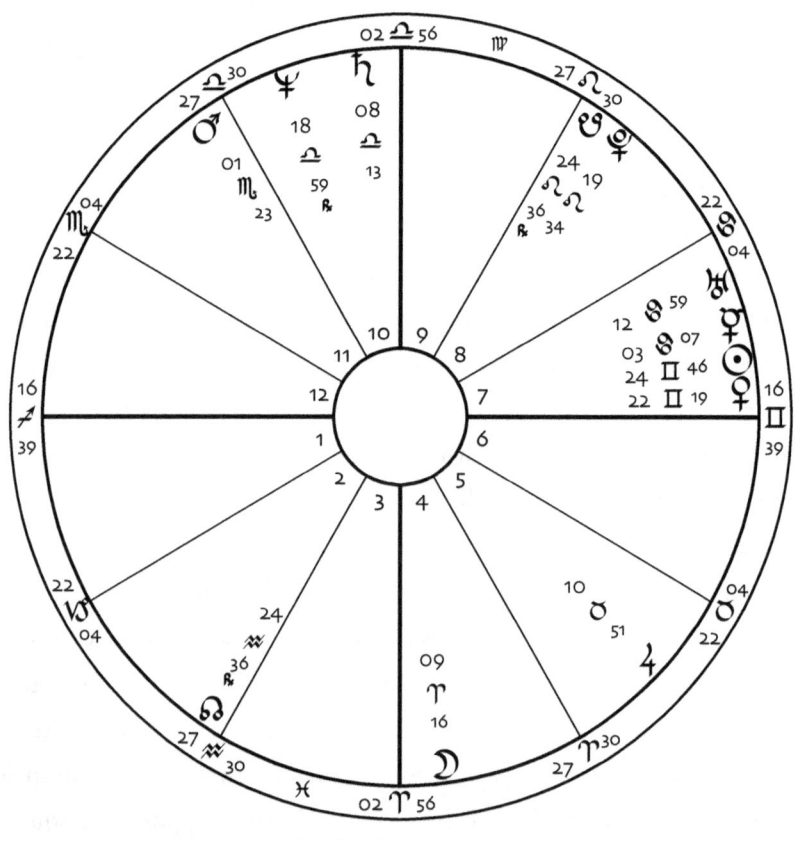

Trudy – June 15, 1952

has worked to overcome blocks to emotional connection with her husband Jack, who often used to brush off her feelings (Moon aspecting Saturn and Uranus). She felt that in parenting she was always the responsible one, while Jack was inconsistent and indulged children's misbehavior (Uranus in the 7th). But no matter, because together they raised three strong and successful individuals, two of them entering the field of business and corporate law (Jupiter, planet of law, in Taurus in the 5th house), and the third owned cattle and became a dairy farmer. Trudy gushed about Jack and what an irrepressible chatterbox and storyteller he was, and what a unique person (Mercury-Uranus conjunction in the 7th house). With Aries Moon in her 4th house, she was an assertive, commanding matriarch in the home, and loved being in the kitchen. With the 4th house Moon—planet of food and cooking—placed in the career–10th house from the husband–7th house, square Uranus in the 7th, Jack is a well-known, trend-setting chef. With the 7th house emphasis of her chart, and Saturn in Libra, her husband, her marriage, and her children were her life, the center of everything. Note that her 7th house Sun and Venus are semi-square Jupiter in the 5th house, showing love and harmony between spouses in relation to children.

Damian

Here is the chart of Damian, whose life also revolves around his family. At age 3, a family tragedy occurred, his father's sudden death, when the solar arc Midheaven opposed Pluto in his 4th house. Pluto is closely conjunct the north node, so this planet's influence was accentuated. With Moon and Mars rising in Cancer, Damian became a feisty, competitive, highly emotional child, a star athlete, and sometimes his temper got the better of him. He always looked after his mother. He met his wife, April, in his late twenties when transiting Saturn-Uranus in Sagittarius were conjunct his Descendant and square natal Venus. The lessons learned during transits can be permanent, and at this time Damian transformed into a loyal, zestful husband and he never looked back. With Sun in the 8th house (house

Astrology as a Therapeutic Art

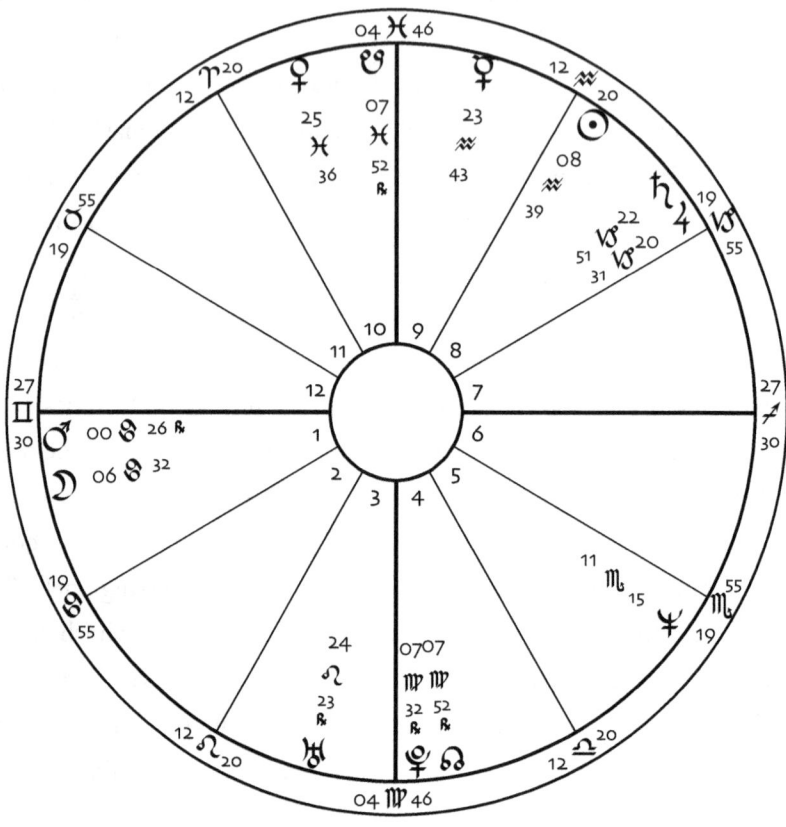

Damian – January 28, 1961

of interpersonal commitments and agreements), widely but unmistakably conjunct Saturn, at his Saturn Return Damian married April, they bought their first house, and they had a child, all within two years. He fully adjusted to his identity as a husband, father, and provider (Sun-Saturn). With Sun semi-square Venus, he's a loving, agreeable, and affectionate spouse and parent. Eventually the couple had two more children. With Moon-Mars conjunction in Cancer, Damian is a caring healthcare professional who works with families, and is an excellent cook. He lives the path of the Moon.

Relationships in Transition: Pathways of Change

It is refreshing for me to meet people, such as Trudy and Damian, who are so well-adjusted in the area of human relationships. In my experience this is also somewhat rare, as many people's interpersonal karma is substantially more complicated!

Gwen

A story comes to mind about stress in the interpersonal field. A woman named Gwen had natal Saturn conjunct the south node in Aquarius, conjunct the IC, and square Neptune at the Ascendant. When Gwen was a child, her mother had mental health issues and Gwen and her two siblings took care of the house, forging their mother's signature on checks to pay

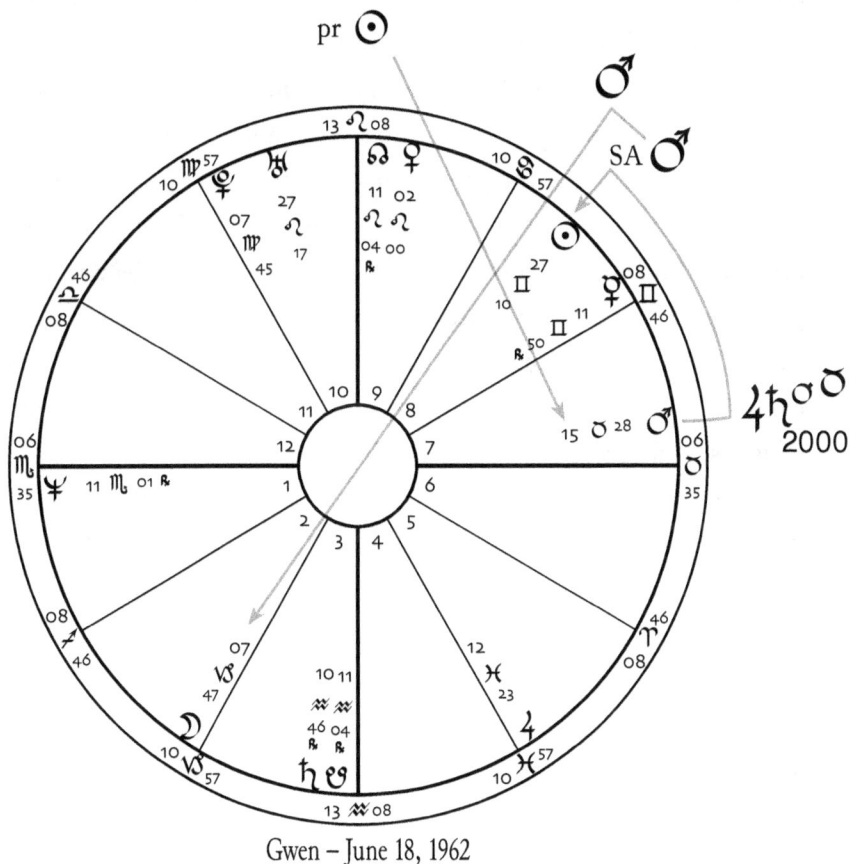

Gwen – June 18, 1962

the bills. From the very beginning, Saturn at the IC represented family and domestic responsibilities. As an adult, she married at age 38 in the year 2000, at the Jupiter-Saturn conjunction in Taurus in her 7th house, a momentous transit. She divorced a few years later, when solar arc Mars was conjunct her 8th house Sun. Her son was 3 years old at that point, and her husband never paid child support (natal Mars in Taurus in the 7th house). She got rather emotional discussing this. The healing power of astrology stems not just from our future predictions (which give us the sense of what is meant to happen) but also from interpreting events in retrospect, shedding light on their underlying meaning. Here I commented how it was likely she'd experience some contentious dynamics and disagreements during solar arc Mars conjunct Sun, and I affirmed how beastly and brutish the husband's behavior was, how selfish and stubborn (Mars in Taurus in the 7th house, square the Moon's nodes and the Midheaven). We can't change other people but it's useful to see them for exactly who they are.

Noting that now, at the present time, at age 48, her progressed Sun was squaring natal Mars, I asked Gwen why she never took her ex-husband to court over the unpaid child support. "I think this would be a way to own your Mars fire and assertiveness, your will power to get what is rightfully yours, at least until your son turns 18." In addition, solar arc Mars was currently opposing Gwen's Moon from the 8th house of divorce, division of assets, and agreements about child or spousal support; this was clearly a time when one would anticipate some heated emotional circumstances. Within weeks of this discussion Gwen did decide to initiate action through her lawyer. At this time Gwen was facing increased stress pertaining to her elderly mother, who was going through many changes, and it was costing Gwen a lot to arrange care. She was also feeling financial pressure because she wanted to send her son to private school. She definitely needed more money. Also, in her role as a corporate administrator, a male employee filed a grievance against Gwen, saying she'd passed him over for a promotion, supposedly because he refused to give her a hug, which was completely bogus; and women in the workplace were up in arms for various reasons. She considered resigning, though she was a few years shy of being fully vested for retirement benefits. With progressed Sun square Mars and solar Mars opposite the Moon, she was passing through a rough phase of life. Here I'm only describing a few progressed contacts involving Mars, and not even mentioning the relevant transits. Discussing these Mars aspects over some weeks evoked several impactful conversations and helped Gwen navigate through the stressors of single parenting, being forced to respond to a grievance against her in the workplace (progressed Sun square the 7th-house Mars: coming under attack), and choosing to pursue legal recourse against her delinquent ex-husband, taking the battle to him like a brave warrior.

Gwen held her ground and kept her job, and after several months the workplace situation calmed down and eventually the storms passed. With her 5th house Jupiter square Mercury in Gemini, throughout this tumultuous period, she always enjoyed talking to her son Taylor. She found his mind and ideas to be so interesting. She said Taylor was already a good writer and her intuition was that he would one day go to college to study journalism. For the time being, Gwen's intelligence and embrace of learning, symbolized by Jupiter square Mercury, was helping shape her son's advanced thinking and communication skills. This was one of her most fulfilling human relationships. She may have had a dishonorable ex-husband but she got a great kid in the bargain.

Rebecca

Rebecca sought me out for marriage counseling, saying that she was very unhappy. With her Sun-Mercury-Uranus conjunction ascending at birth, she is a funny, witty person who easily makes other people laugh. With Mars-Pluto in Virgo, Rebecca is fit and strong and works out intensely, but she has suffered several injuries due to overzealous workouts. Previously divorced, she received strong material and financial support from the 8th

Astrology as a Therapeutic Art

house Saturn in Taurus and from her recent marriage to Sam, a commercial building contractor, and they bought a house together (Taurus planets in the house of shared finances). With her 8th house Moon-Saturn conjunction in Taurus, the material aspects of the marriage and the state of their joint bank accounts and investments were a major focus of her attention.

Mars and Pluto are in her 12th house, the house of solitude, but it's also the 6th house from the partner–7th house and thus the house of the spouse's work and workplace, and also the spouse's health. Rebecca said Sam was a very hard worker, and that the strain of his physically demanding work was affecting his health. "He's always working, making money, a workhorse." I said, "I imagine that when Sam is occupied at work you might feel quite

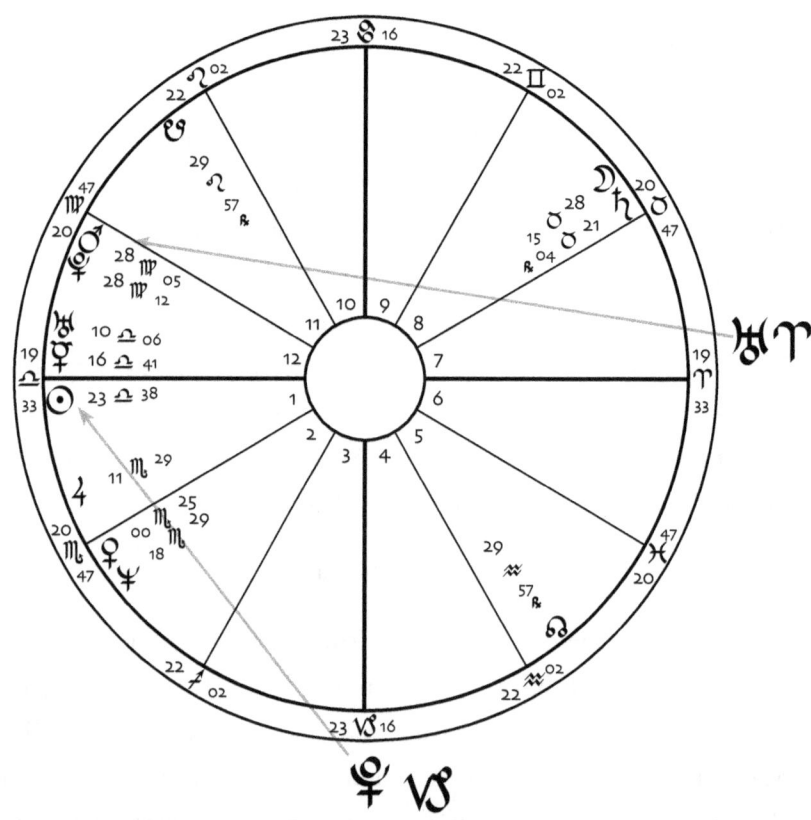

Rebecca – October 17, 1970

alone and also somewhat anxious because of Mars in Virgo." Rebecca said he'd sometimes be away for long periods at work sites and she'd start to feel abandoned and resentful. Mars in Virgo showed her tendency toward excessive worry and anxiety, which built up to a high degree of tension when Sam was out of town for weeks at a time working on construction projects, and she held a lot of simmering anger about his absence. So she picked fights and constantly expressed dissatisfaction with him (7th house dispositor Mars conjunct Pluto in Virgo). She complained that Sam was very critical and even somewhat mean to her. But the critic was also embedded inside her, in her unconscious (12th house), and she fixated on internal criticisms and imaginary attacks. Throughout her life, her father's criticism had been relentless, and now she interpreted Sam's absence as tacit criticism. That was the story she told about it—that he was spending time away from her because she was worthless and inadequate. She had a lot of fantasies that Sam was having an affair and a secret life in remote locations (Mars-Pluto in the 12th house, realm of the imagination). So she kept a lot of rage bottled up inside her, adopting an outward demeanor that was tense and emotionally guarded. That reminded Rebecca of her mother, who was emotionally stingy and cold, signified by the Moon-Saturn conjunction, square the nodal axis. She said, "I'm shocked at how much I've been acting like my mom lately." Rebecca described withdrawing emotionally and withholding sex from Sam, which was causing a lot of sadness and whining on his part. Contemplating her Moon square the nodes, I wondered out loud, What was she feeling most deeply? With Mars, ruler of the 7th house, in the 12th house, she said she was experiencing intense loneliness. On the other hand, the 12th house symbolism seemed to indicate the importance of tolerating periods of solitude.

At the time of consultation, transiting Uranus in Aries had recently crossed her Descendant and entered her 7th house, and was forming a quincunx to natal Mars. When Uranus is active, events can take surprising, unexpected turns and twists, all of a sudden. With Uranus at the Descendant changes occur in the interpersonal sphere. At the same time, transiting Pluto in Capricorn squared her Libra Sun, bringing complications in her relational life as Rebecca developed a growing attraction to another man. Rebecca said, "Sam surprised me with flowers the other day and was uncharacteristically affectionate. It was completely out of the blue. But I'm confused right now because I have feelings for somebody else." Under the impetus of these transits, for several months she carried on a secret affair with Chris, her yoga teacher, who was married. In this way she was living out the sexually intense, explosive, orgasmic potentials of natal Mars conjunct Pluto, releasing energies that had long been dormant. The problem was the emotional cost of keeping the relationship with Chris hidden, suppressed, and out of view. She was living a truly 12th house type of existence. She felt a lot of intense guilt as she knew she was disregarding her agreements with Sam, and rationalizing this. After all, she told herself, who knew what Sam was up to on his business trips?

All of this was increasing, not decreasing, her level of anxiety. It occurred to me that her Moon-Saturn in the 8th house meant that she needed to exhibit a high degree of emotional integrity. I said, "It's one thing to have had this affair and this exciting experience under the impetus of Uranus conjunct your Descendant, quincunx natal Mars, and also Pluto square your Sun. So far you've been able to keep the affair with Chris under wraps. It's another thing to keep it going and to risk eventually destroying both marriages. Even if you were unattached, remember that Chris is married. He is off limits. He's taken. He's what American football players call 'an ineligible receiver.'"

Rebecca absorbed this comment and said, "I haven't been thinking clearly. I've always been a very ethical person. I know Sam would be furious and hurt if he knew what's going on while he's out of town. And I don't want any of that. This is probably the worst thing I've ever done in my life, and you're probably right that it's best to not keep it going."

I'm not saying it's easy to stay sexually interested in the same person for years or decades, or to avoid other attractions and to remain monogamous. Situations arise, transits happen, and people sometimes can't help themselves. But these "stolen moments" can initiate a process that gets out of control. I once saw a case where a single kiss with a coworker in a back room at the office led to a divorce that turned upside down the lives of a couple, their in-laws, siblings, neighbors, and relatives.

With her Pluto square her Libra Sun on the Ascendant Rebecca realized that the relationship with Sam was worth preserving, and she consciously sacrificed the relationship with Chris and broke off the affair. Pluto transits sometimes mark irrevocable endings. She and Chris had genuine feelings for each other but this was one of those situations in life that just cannot be. And that is exactly what I suggested she say to Chris: This cannot be. At the time she chose not to tell Sam about Chris and kept it a secret because she feared the consequences. But she decided to put out the fire before it consumed everything. She'd already been through a divorce caused by infidelity. Sooner or later everyone does things that in retrospect we realize may have been a mistake. What's important is whether we keep making the same mistake or whether we make a course correction. It reminds me of Louis and Conrad and their decision to cut down their excessive wine sipping. It's within our power to make intelligent behavioral shifts that will bring about beneficial changes in our lives and our evolutionary trajectory.

Freya

Some transits clearly indicate periods that are likely to be stressful in the relational domain. Freya, age 29, had Saturn and Pluto transit over her Descendant and then conjoined natal Uranus and Neptune in her 7th house. Freya felt the emergence of toxicity and hostility in her relationship with her best friend, Ariel, and severed contact after they had a sudden falling out. Ariel had returned to the underworld of addiction—abusing booze and cocaine, acting erratically, and hooking up randomly with guys at bars

Astrology as a Therapeutic Art

(Pluto conjunct Uranus-Neptune in the 7th). She and Ariel had partied together for several years, drinking and ingesting various drugs at nightclubs, but now Freya didn't feel like going out anymore, and she was shocked to see the disorganized, disheveled condition of her friend. With her natal Sun-Venus conjunction in Cancer, at the Ascendant, Freya was emotionally attached to friends and never wanted to lose anyone, but with natal Sun-Venus opposite Uranus-Neptune she'd always been drawn to a social circle of unruly, zany, druggie, boozy people. Under this Pluto transit to these planets, she felt the urge and the imperative to break away. She was done with that life. Pluto is the power of repudiation and renunciation and the instinct to detoxify. Ariel's behavior had become so unpredictable

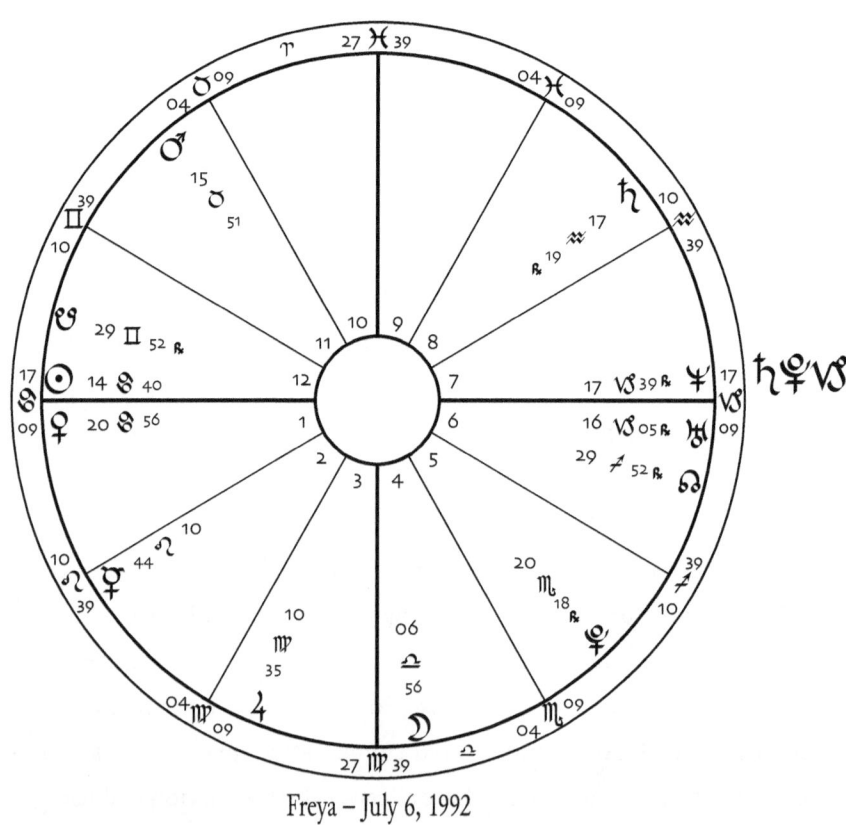

Freya – July 6, 1992

and unsettling that Freya's sense of trust and closeness with her friend had broken, and trust is crucial for a person with Sun in the sign of Cancer. Commenting on Pluto crossing the Descendant and conjunct Uranus and Neptune, I said, "I think you've outgrown the friendship with Ariel. You're molting it like an old skin that no longer fits." At the same time, with Pluto conjunct her Descendant she was initiated into Vajrayana Buddhism and Tibetan tantric *ngondro* practices and purifications, and she became associated with a group of Tibetan Buddhist Lamas and practitioners. With this transit, life brought Freya to a definitive parting of the ways, and she chose a path of transformation.

Drew

In our role as astrologers people tell us stories that sometimes stay with us for years to come. Thirty years ago I consulted with a client who worked through a somewhat difficult, intense natal configuration. Drew was born with Moon (planet of the mother) conjunct Saturn and Pluto in Leo, opposite Sun, Venus, Mars, and Mercury in Aquarius. With the Full Moon conjunct Saturn and Pluto, Drew was gestated and born while her mother was in a locked psychiatric ward, and she was raised initially by nurses in the ward. Her mother was schizophrenic and remained institutionalized on and off for the rest of her life. Deep emotional conflicts began to manifest in adolescence at the Saturn opposition, when Drew became suicidal and engaged in various self-harming behaviors, and she also became somewhat male-identified, got involved with boxing and weight-lifting, and was assertive in sexually pursuing other women (Sun-Mars conjunction). For decades she had relationships with various women, always, as she put it, "looking for my mom."

In 1988, with transiting Uranus and Saturn in Sagittarius conjunct her natal Venus she got involved with a man (named William) for the first time at age 41, and underwent a change of sexual orientation and identity. A crisis was reached three years later, in 1991, during a Jupiter-Saturn opposition, with transiting Saturn conjunct Sun-Venus-Mars in Aquarius and transiting Jupiter in Leo conjunct Moon-Saturn-Pluto. During these impactful transits she experienced a great deal of anger in the relationship with William, to the point where she physically assaulted him on two occasions. Then she became panicked and suicidal when her psychotherapist emotionally abandoned her, saying she couldn't handle Drew's intense rage, which kept flaring up while transiting Jupiter and Saturn activated her Sun-Mars opposite Moon, Pluto, and Saturn. The therapist had the nerve to say to Drew that her egotism and indignant acting out were insufferable. This episode highlights the traumatic nature of some interpersonal relations when discordant elements are present in the 7th house.

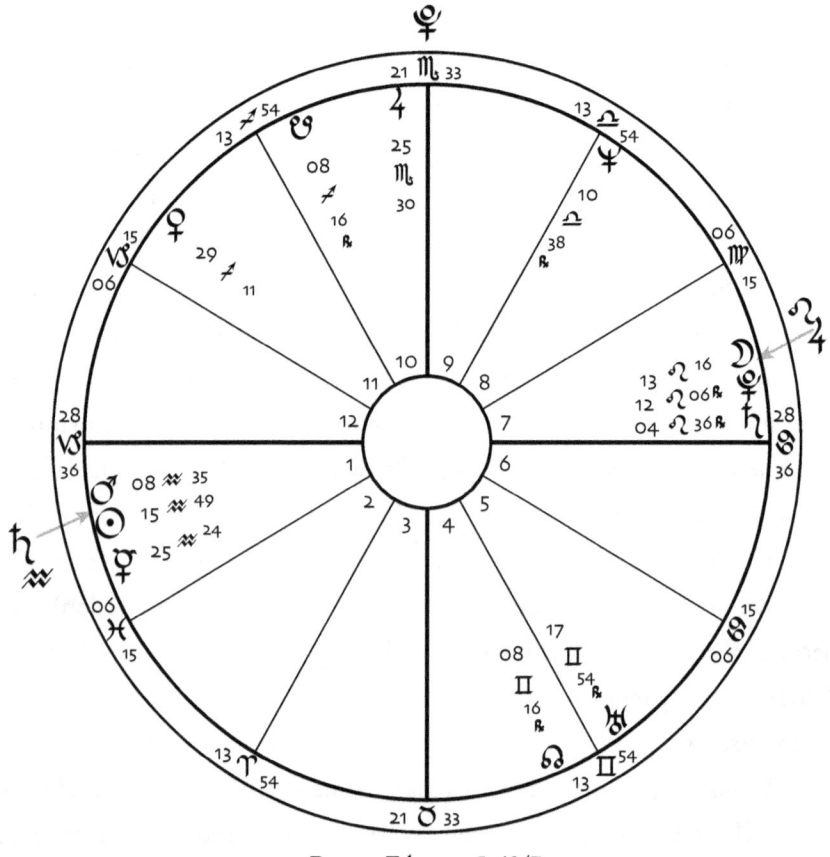

Drew – February 5, 1947

The rupture of this counseling relationship felt like a shattering repetition of the original wound about her mother's unavailability. During transits to the Moon we touch our deepest feelings, which may include sadness over unmet needs, and also guilt and a longing for emotional reparation. In the end this crisis became the decisive moment of change in her life. Drew had the healthy, adaptive instinct to look for help to see her through this upheaval, so she found another therapist who emotionally adopted her and sustained her so she could begin to self-regulate. While Jupiter was conjunct Moon-Saturn-Pluto several huge emotional outbursts and catharses magnified her awareness of feelings and past incidents that were the source of her seething anger, and she began to express to William how specific actions and words offended her and showed disrespect, a key concern for Moon in Leo. She realized that he was very receptive to this feedback and that she didn't have to be so dramatic and volcanic in expressing this. With the support of William and this new therapist (while transiting Jupiter in Leo passed through her 7th house) she began to experience deeper self-respect and to appreciate her emotional strength and maturity, which had enabled her to survive her mother's mental illness and become self-sufficient. Saturn-Pluto aspects often indicate a need to develop strength and toughness to endure arduous circumstances and adversities, and to be a survivor. As a child Drew had been a brave little soldier and now she felt proud of herself. She came to understand her insecure-ambivalent attachment patterns and the huffy, aggressive behavior that got provoked by her fear of abandonment. She recognized the destructive consequences of her violent, histrionic, explosive episodes, and her oversensitivity to perceived slights. By the final pass of the Jupiter-Saturn opposition, she married William and had two children with him within three years, in her early forties. I witnessed how the Jupiter-Saturn transit awakened her instinct for marriage and children, shown by natal Sun-Mars semi-square Venus, Sun trine Uranus in the child–5th house, and also her 7th house Leo Moon. Drew went through a complete metamorphosis and worked

Astrology as a Therapeutic Art

extremely hard to gain emotional maturity and to establish the family life she ultimately chose to create with William. With natal Jupiter in the 10th house, she became a clinical psychologist, experiencing much professional growth and expansion beginning in 1992 when Pluto in Scorpio passed over her Midheaven and natal Jupiter. An amazing, magnetic, influential, and fully unfolded person emerged from a very intense birth chart.

Sara

Sara had Sun, Pluto, and Venus square Mars in Scorpio in the 7th house. She said, "Men dominate me," and she perceived men as arrogant, selfish, and gratuitously mean and insensitive. That describes perfectly how it felt

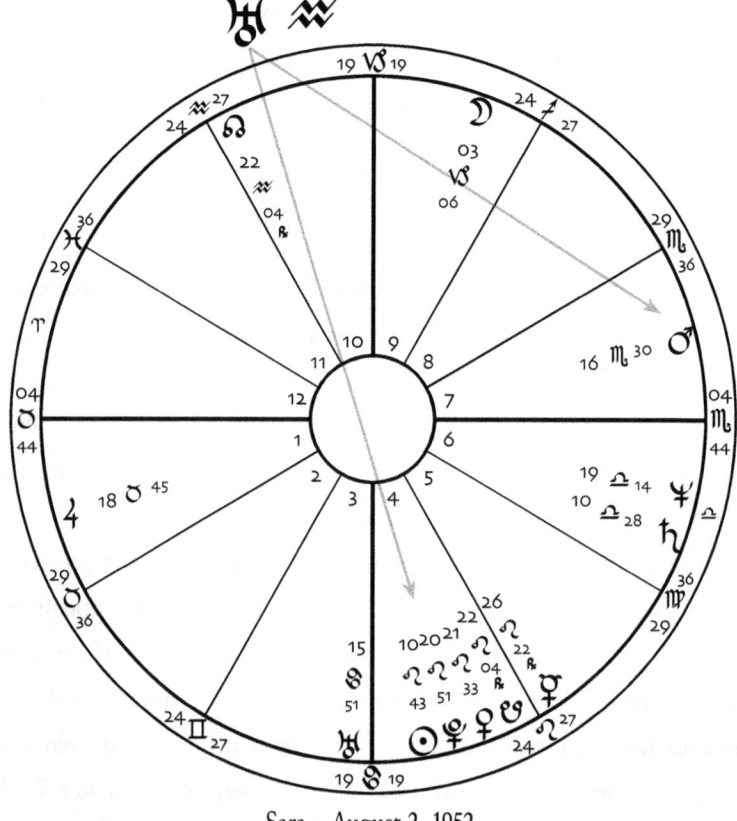

Sara – August 2, 1952

to her to have Mars setting in Scorpio, near the Descendant, the point of impactful relatedness. She wanted to let herself be very strong and dominant in her relationships but said she feared being perceived as a bitch. That statement encapsulates the feeling of having Sun square Mars and an instinct to stand up for herself and to be very blunt, but at the same time, with Sun-Venus conjunction, she would like to be very nice about it.

At the time of consultation Uranus in Aquarius was forming a Grand Cross, square Mars, square Jupiter, and opposite Sun-Pluto. She said, "I'm involved with a man, Jim, who keeps saying he doesn't want to be in an exclusive relationship with me. We recently had several dramatic breakups." Mars-Uranus energy can be a volatile mix and one can be susceptible to outbursts of anger and inflamed situations. Uranus, representing an urge for freedom and change, was activating the powerful Sun-Pluto conjunction in Leo, and natal Mars in Scorpio. A clash, or some act of personal liberation, seemed inevitable. It was insulting to her that Jim wanted to be with other women. It was an injury to her pride. She hated him for that. But with her Leo Sun, she held herself in high enough esteem to not stand for it. After several breakups with Jim, Sara ended up hooking up with a guy she met at a Vegas casino and they had a shotgun wedding at an Elvis chapel. She got into some freaky sex with Casino Man, but the last I heard it hadn't worked out between them and she had the marriage annulled. It seemed that Sara needed to have that experience with Uranus square Mars, and opposite the Sun, to exhaust that karma. Not every relationship has to be a long-term agreement. She felt that this tumultuous episode finally enabled her to disentangle herself from Jim, so it wasn't all bad. Her Sun-Venus-Pluto in Leo represented a need for attention, admiration, and demonstrations of love and loyalty that could never be satisfied by a relationship with someone who was ambivalent about her. With Venus in Leo conjunct the south node, she was a very attractive person who drew lots of interest and had plenty of options, so her relational quest continued.

Tricia

Tricia, an American woman living in a Middle East country, had an unusual dilemma when transiting Saturn in Pisces opposed her natal Venus in Virgo. Over the previous year, with Saturn transiting her 7th house, she formed a relationship with a Muslim man who wanted to marry her, but he had another wife, who was not happy about Tricia becoming wife number two. It's common in his culture for men to have more than one wife, but the first wife felt threatened by Tricia and was resistant to the new arrangement and the new reality. So even though Tricia and her fiancé Ahmed had a joining ceremony, he hadn't followed through with the legal

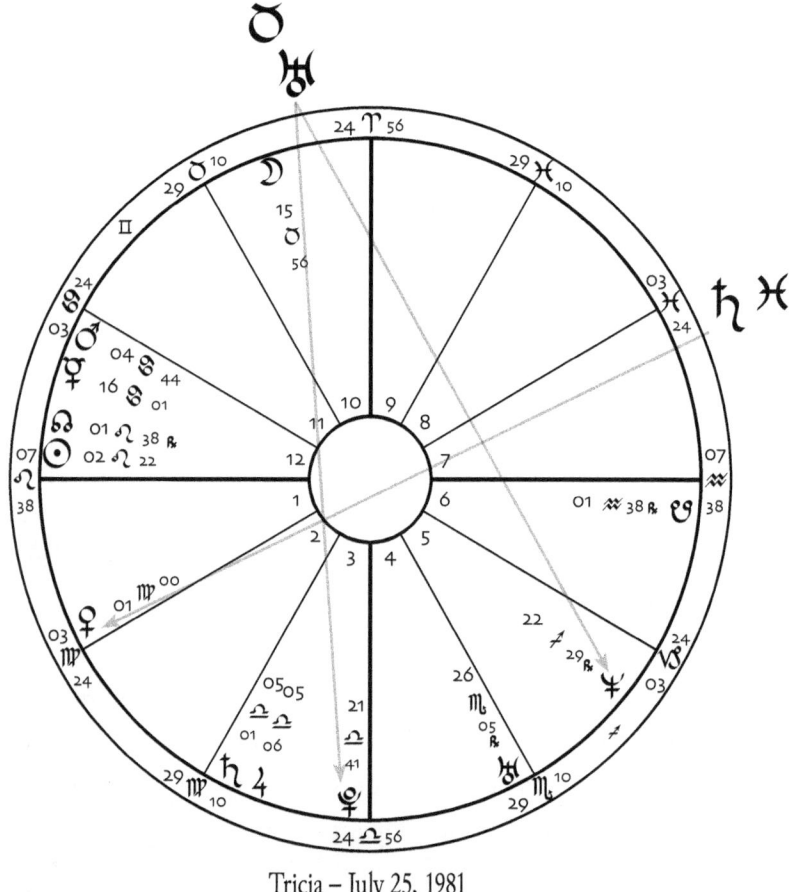

Tricia – July 25, 1981

marriage, and he hadn't told his parents about her yet. Tricia faced uncertainty about the marriage contract and their commitment, and she was afraid of being abandoned. Transiting Uranus in Taurus was forming a Yod with Pluto and Neptune. Uranus quincunx Pluto in Libra in the 4th house showed the complicated family situation, and her feeling unsettled and displaced living in a foreign country, without a secure home. With Uranus quincunx natal Neptune, her situation was fuzzy, ambiguous, and undefined, with no solid ground. For Tricia this was an ordeal of suffering due to a situation not completely in her control. I said, "I think you're being tested, and going through a process that requires trust, surrender, and letting go." With transiting Saturn now entering her 8th house, she was financially dependent on Ahmed. Noting that transiting Saturn in Pisces was going to turn stationary direct in a few months, exactly opposing natal Venus in Virgo, I said, "This is a time when you're likely to want greater certainty, definition, and commitment in this relationship. That's the nature of a Venus-Saturn aspect. You want the emotional and financial security of being legally married, and you want the marriage to become an established pillar of your life structure." Several months later, as Saturn turned stationary direct, Tricia wrote to tell me that Ahmed decided to legally marry her and he had initiated a divorce from his first wife.

Martha

Martha had Sun in the 5th house, square Saturn in the 3rd house of speech and elocution. A former actress who had spent much of her early life in the performing arts (5th house Sun), she was now doing a lot of public speaking for her church, but sometimes while speaking in public she felt tightness in her throat (Saturn in 3rd house) and froze up in front of her audience. She experienced a lot of self-doubt about whether she knew enough about theology and whether people would find her talks interesting. In actual fact, people told her she was captivating yet unassuming, and they valued her willingness to show her vulnerability. Sun and Mercury in the 5th house

Astrology as a Therapeutic Art

showed talent and identity through the creative expression of theater. Transiting Pluto was currently conjunct her Sun and she was now experiencing a rebirth of the actress, just on a different kind of stage. With Neptune in her 4th house, she lived in her dream home near the ocean with a large swimming pool in the back yard. The 4th house is also the career–10th house from the husband–7th house, and with Neptune placed here her husband was a film producer who moved among the beautiful and rich celebrities of Hollywood. With Pisces on her MC, and its ruler, Neptune, conjunct Venus, she was a fundraiser for her spiritual community and felt that service in this role was one of her most treasured accomplishments. With her Moon-Pluto conjunction in Leo in her 2nd house, she knew how

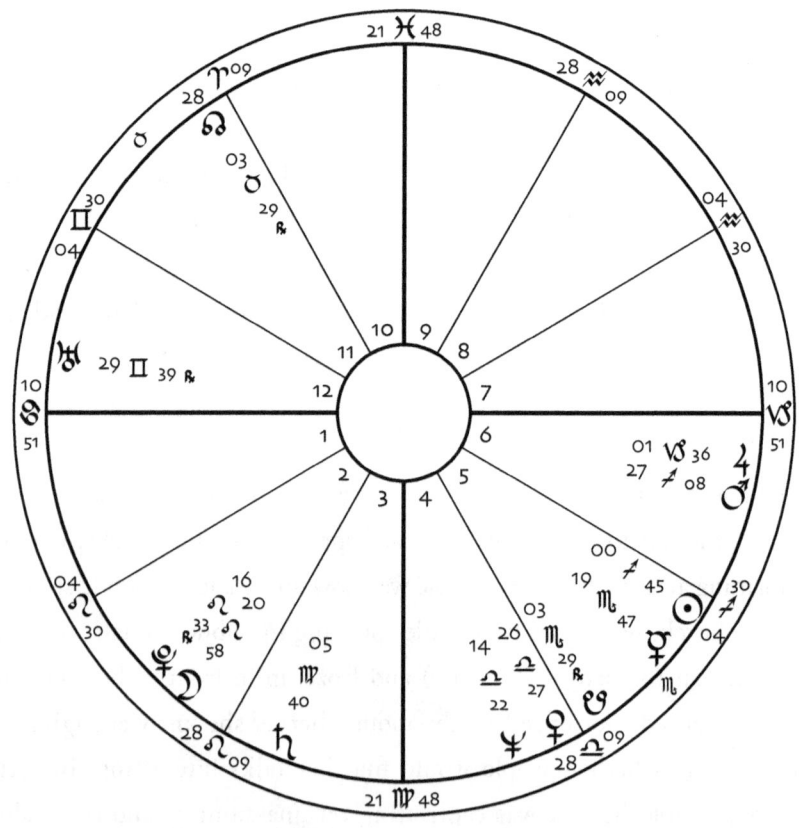

Martha – November 22, 1948

to raise large amounts of money. The mother of three, she has gone through immense changes in life as a mother. For example, when transiting Pluto was conjunct her 5th-house Sun, her two daughters both went through a crisis and started to have panic attacks and episodes of derealization and dissociation. They did come through this over the course of time and both of them advanced through pursuing postgraduate education (Pluto conjunct Sun in Sagittarius). The 2nd house is also the 8th house from husband–7th, so it rules the husband's business and financial agreements. Through this business they amassed a good amount of wealth as a couple.

In 1999, the transiting square of Saturn in Taurus and Uranus in Aquarius aspected natal Moon-Pluto, and her husband became involved in controversy about the sale of his film production company and the couple was in danger of financial ruin. They geared up for war and spent a fortune on legal fees, and eventually reached a settlement. At this time, Uranus in Aquarius opposed the Moon and squared her Mercury in Scorpio in the 5th house, and her daughter was tough and sarcastic, and talked about sex constantly. There were various emotional family dramas and upsets. With Uranus opposite Moon, she was opening up as a mother, becoming less uptight, more open-minded; her daughter wanted to explore her sexuality, and Martha had to accept this. She refocused her energies on fundraising for the church, a role she assumed in the year 2000 during the Jupiter-Saturn conjunction in Taurus in the 11th house, making an immense commitment to group activity. The 11th house is also the 7th house from the child–5th house and thus governs a child's relationships, and this was the time when her daughter got involved with her first serious boyfriend.

Davi

Davi has Uranus and Pluto conjunct the north node in Virgo in the 4th house. Both her parents grew up poor and her father was quite controlling and somewhat dangerous and unpredictable. With this kind of energy in the 4th house natally one can expect various family crises. The Sun squares

Pluto with an orb of 3 ½ degrees, and at age 3 her mother was ill and nearly died. At the same time Davi's maternal grandmother was staying with the family and was demanding and needy. Another crisis occurred at age 12–13, when solar arc Uranus was conjunct Pluto. Her mother was critically ill again and had an emergency hysterectomy. "I was home alone when I was told my mom could die. That was a wakeup call." Davi became a physical therapist who works in pain management and recovery (Uranus and Pluto in Virgo, zodiacal sign of healthcare). When her progressed Sun reached her Descendant at age 20 she went to university, made new friends, and had her first boyfriend. She met her husband Austin six years later when the progressed Sun was conjunct Jupiter in Capricorn in the 7th house. They

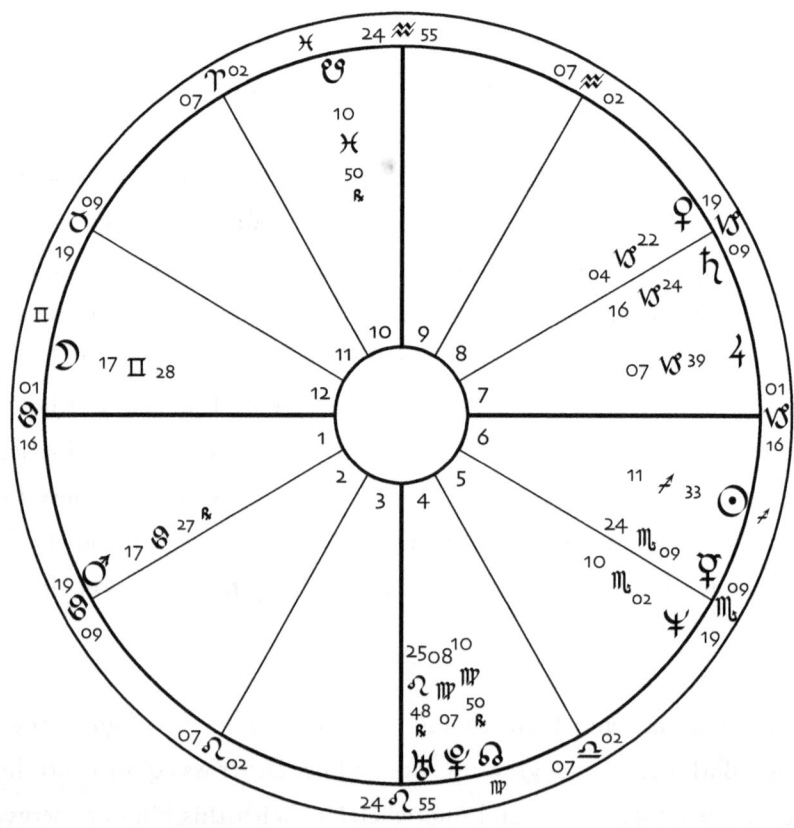

Davi – December 3, 1960

met in graduate school (Jupiter: education). The 4th house is the career–10th house from the husband–7th, and with Uranus, the planet of science and technology, conjunct Pluto, planet of engineering, placed here, Austin has degrees in physics and electrical engineering. With her Jupiter in Capricorn in the 7th house, they formed a marriage of professionals, where both of them remained dedicated to their careers.

Years later, in 2010, when solar arc Mars was conjunct Pluto in her 4th house, Davi's father died, she liquidated his house and belongings, and she bought a small property with the money. She and Austin have now retired, and with her 4th house emphasis, natal Mars in Cancer opposing Saturn, and Ascendant ruler Moon rising at birth, they are now fully in their element, spending much of their time working on their house and property, taking care of pets, removing dead trees and clearing debris from their land, regenerating the soil with compost, and growing a healthy vegetable garden.

Lily

I once gave a client some astrological advice that helped revive a relationship. Lily had Sun and Venus conjunct the north node in Cancer in the 11th house. At the start of the session she said that her boyfriend Fred had recently asked her to marry him, but he was apparently preoccupied with his teenage daughter. She said, "I can't compete with his daughter, so I broke it off and stepped out of the relationship. It was overwhelming. I can't deal with living with other people's children. I don't want to be a stepmother. I've never had to deal with other people's kids and ex-spouses." I explained to Lily that her chart featured Sun-Venus in the 11th house, which is the 5th house from the partner–7th house, and thus the house of the partner's children—stepchildren. The 5th house refers to one's own children, but the 11th house refers to any offspring of one's spouse. I told Lily that the chart indicated that if she wanted to be married to Fred, there was a good chance she could establish an affectionate, loving relationship

Astrology as a Therapeutic Art

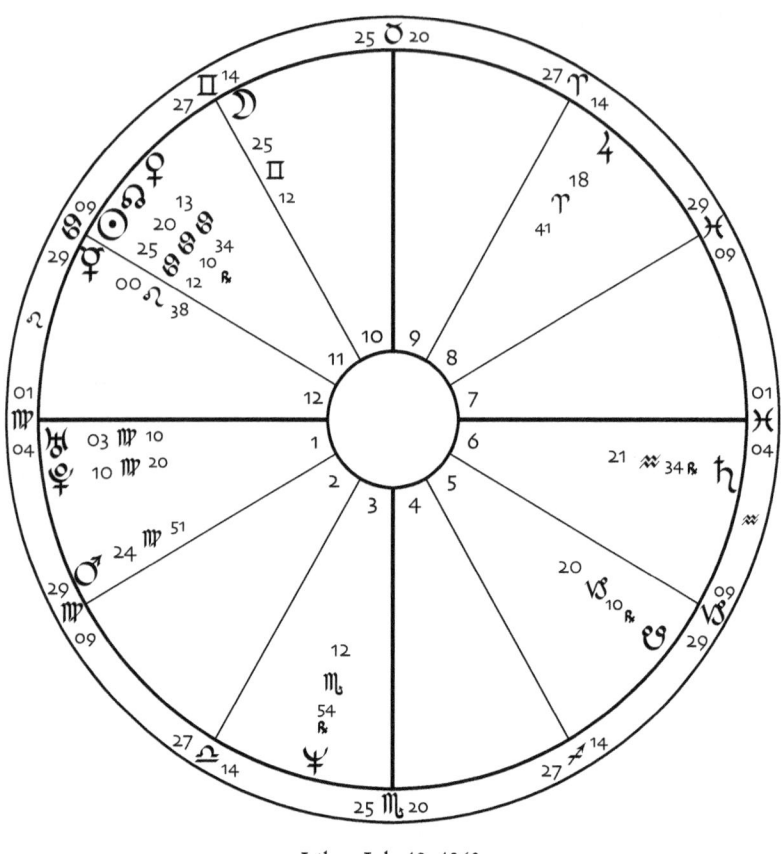

Lily – July 18, 1963

with his child. In fact, she might be very good at step-parenting. Undoubtedly it's emotionally complex to form a blended family, but that's not necessarily a reason not to do it. Lily later married Fred, became a loving stepmother, and had a rewarding experience of family (Sun-Venus in Cancer).

Ted

The next example describes my conversation with Ted, age 69, who has Sun in the 5th house of creativity, closely semi-square Venus and Neptune in Libra. He is an artistic personality who loves to write and paint, a connoisseur of theatre and fine furniture, and he is also a romantic idealist

Relationships in Transition: Pathways of Change

on a lifelong quest for the Beloved through numerous relationships with men, and many disappointments. With Jupiter-Uranus square Venus-Neptune, he is popular and attracts friends readily. With Midheaven ruler Saturn conjunct the Moon in Scorpio, his work in life involves connecting closely to people, and he brings a high degree of emotional sensitivity, empathy, and attunement to his professional alliance with clients. The Scorpio Moon-Saturn signified themes of aggression, force, or emotional cruelty in his relationships with other men, beginning with his father, who doled out corporal punishment, disciplining his two sons with belts and switches to show them who was boss. Ted has devoted years of psychotherapy to address the emotional injuries stemming from this paternal cruelty and

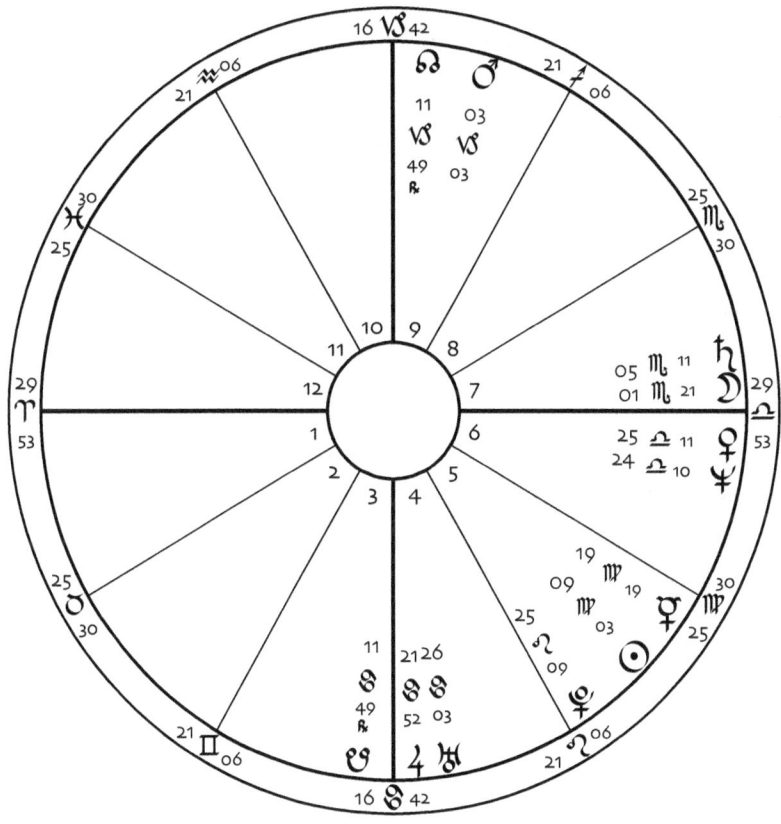

Ted – September 1, 1954

abusive behavior, signified by Saturn in Scorpio. Discussing the Moon-Saturn conjunction, Ted said, "I was deeply bonded with my mother. She smothered me with love. I became a surrogate partner with her, because of my emotional acumen. Because of my close relationship with her I think I developed an expanded emotional range."

At the time of consultation Ted was involved in relationships with three different people, and with one man in particular, Fredo, he'd been exploring some kinky BDSM sex practices. He said, "Domination and submission have come into conscious play, and it awakened me to the fact of eros in the emotional field with my father. I found someone safe for me, and I've been following my own erotic nature and it has really helped. I've discovered myself as a sexual being at a new level. It has been revelatory. I've come to realize that I was always in love with my father. Fredo and I had 17 sessions together, which were a life-transforming peak experience." I said, "You've transformed through engaging the energies of love and aggression, exploring sexuality and power. The way you describe this, it sounds like a spiritual, mystical, erotic religious experience joining pain and ecstasy." Ted commented that this had satisfied his voracious need for emotional connection.

Finally, Ted reported a recent breakthrough: "Recently I told Fredo, 'I don't want to be hit anymore.' I discovered the 4-year-old in me that can finally say, 'Daddy, don't hit me.' I feel great empowerment in saying this. Now there is more equality and mutuality and authenticity in this relationship than I've felt in a long time. There's more pleasure, less pain." This occurred during a time when transiting Pluto in late Capricorn squared his Ascendant/Descendant axis and his natal Venus-Neptune. He was turning away from violence, submission, and masochism toward a more expansive experience of affection and tenderness.

Relationships in Transition: Pathways of Change

Natalia

Natalia, age 45, consulted me twice. In our first conversation she was very interested in finding a life partner but had stopped dating for several years during the Covid pandemic. With Venus in Taurus along with Mercury at her Midheaven she made good money as a project manager. But she was very concerned that she wasn't married. Sun opposite Pluto in Libra represented the fact that she'd become quite mistrustful. She said, "I was in a longer-term relationship when I was younger. I hid him from my family for six years. I was lying to my family because my boyfriend was from an ethnic group my parents didn't approve of. But it turned out he

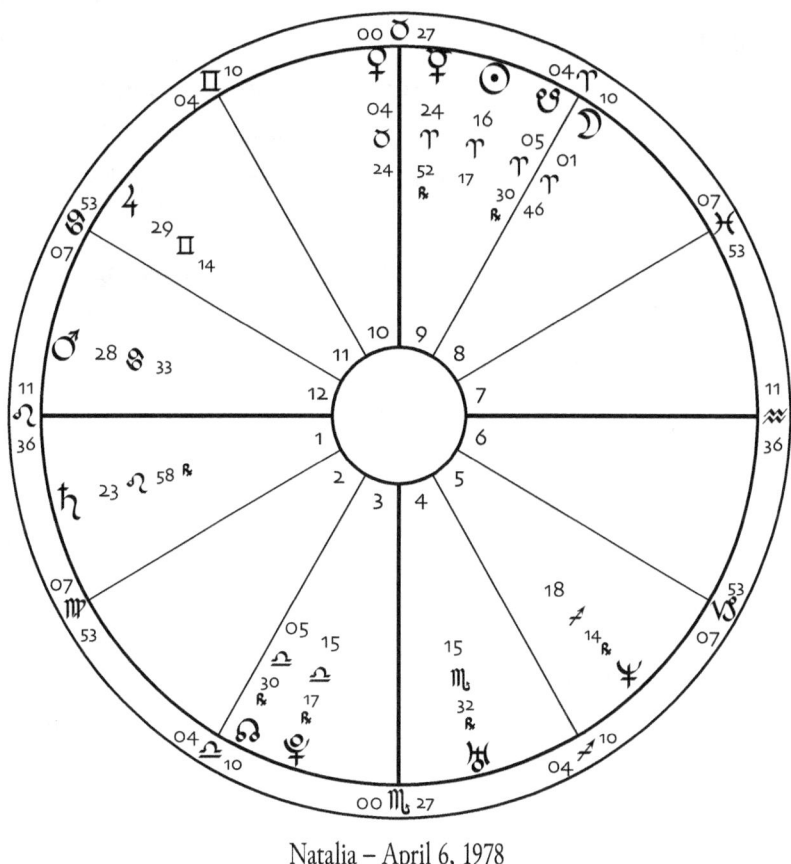

Natalia – April 6, 1978

was in another relationship and cheated on me. I regret that I was ever with him, and I've punished myself a lot for getting myself in that situation. How could I have been such a fool?" Here Sun opposite Pluto in Libra signified a controversial relationship that she kept buried and that ended in betrayal. Also, Pluto is placed in her 3rd house (siblings) and she noted, "My sister and I went through some intense years when we hated each other. But we've put all that to rest now and we've healed." Commenting on the Sun-Pluto, I said, "It sounds like you're ruthless with yourself, blaming yourself for what happened with the secret boyfriend. But also you seem to have become somewhat wary and guarded toward people." She said, "It takes me a long time to trust anyone." "You were injured by that relationship. Your discovery of his affair was traumatic and so you've built armor around yourself. You've stopped dating and are fearful of attempting another relationship due to this deep mistrust. But I encourage you to try again because Venus is strong in Taurus and culminating at your Midheaven, so a relationship is one of your ultimate goals. Therefore I think you should definitely try again and not give up on finding love."

The second consultation occurred two years later, during a time of relational conflict while transiting Pluto was opposing natal Mars in Cancer, in the 12th house. Her new boyfriend Cameron was having stress regarding his anger in the workplace (Mars in the workplace–6th house from the 7th). She said, "He doesn't feel recognized at work and is angry at his manager. So he comes home and lashes out at me. And that triggers me and I get angry too. Usually my anger is hidden; I learned in my family to keep it all suppressed. But now I feel like I could burst. Lots of anger is coming up for both of us, and he starts yelling and screaming and expressing all this resentment toward me." I noted that Mars in Cancer sometimes indicates family discord, emotional upset, and domestic stress, and Natalia said, "There were always family disagreements. For example, when I broke up with that guy I'd kept hidden, my parents found out about him and were outraged and there was a big family crisis. Now the domestic stress stems from the fact that Cameron doesn't come to my place. I always go to his apartment. It's all on his terms. And his reactions are out of line. His words hurt. I've never felt so lonely." I said "It's important not to shut down because of the heated emotions. While Pluto is opposite Mars, the mood of the relationship probably isn't going to feel soft and calm and sensitive right now. There's a raw emotional atmosphere. But if you're this angry at each other maybe it means that deep down you both really care."

Natalia told me, "The current stressor in the relationship is that I want to live together. He doesn't want to. He wants to keep his man cave." I said, "Saturn has been transiting through your 7th house over this past year while the relationship has formed, and it was also during your Saturn opposition, so I think you take it very seriously, and you want this to work out. You want to experience a full union with him, which for you would mean cohabiting or possibly getting married at some point. And I notice that Jupiter in Taurus is conjunct your natal Venus this fall. I want you to focus on that and feel hopeful. Don't give up on Cameron. Just let him know how you feel about him and that you want him in your life for a long time to come. He'd be a fool not to respond favorably to that, and if he doesn't, then he clearly doesn't deserve you."

I don't know where this story ends yet but I feel satisfied that our analysis of her astrological situation gave Natalia hope and affirmed her sense of purpose and commitment to the relationship. Throughout this book we've noted how the study of planetary cycles and symbols can strengthen the resolve to persevere in our efforts to create loving, trusting connections. It can help people understand each other's charts, each other's needs, and each other's character. Knowledge of planetary transits can aid people confronting crisis and the storms of life together. Astrological study brings into focus crucial seasons of marriages and friendships, attractions and breakups, the recurrence of unconscious projections, and the need to change our behavior toward others, thus altering our destiny.

Chapter 5

Concluding Thoughts

I firmly believe that astrotherapeutic work is going to become increasingly popular in the future. I can imagine what a difference it would make if more psychotherapists studied astrology, and I'm hoping that the examples in this volume demonstrate to therapists, in practical terms, how astrology can inform and deepen and enlighten their clinical practice. In this book I demonstrate my own approach to astrological marriage and family therapy and recount stories that show the value of using astrology to address issues such as neurotic anger or avoidance, alcohol abuse, affairs and addictions, and conflicts about sex and intimacy.

Practitioners of the future will combine astrology with gestalt therapy, psychoanalysis, psychosynthesis, dance and art therapies, holotropic breathwork, yoga therapy, narrative therapy, dialectical behavioral therapy, and Jungian analysis and psychotherapy. I find this last avenue especially interesting, as my work with clients is greatly enhanced by referring to C. G. Jung's principles of individuation, dialogue with the unconscious, ego-Self alignment, resolving complexes, unfolding a multiplicity of archetypal transformations, and the achievement of wholeness through the union of opposites. For me personally, the ultimate meeting point of astrology and psychology is through the union of astrology and dreams; we saw an example of this in the story of Jorge, and the practice of astrological dreamwork is explored at length in *Astrology's Higher Octaves*. In all of these varied forms, I think we have the basis for transformative, holistic spiritual psychotherapies. It would be amazing if one day this work were as commonplace as the use of psychiatric medications.

I believe that all astrologers can apply astropsychological principles to aid their self-understanding and to resolve emotional injuries and issues causing interpersonal discord in various realms of life. Astrologers can begin to think in therapeutic ways and interpret chart symbols in the light of developmental stages, personality traits, emotional attachment, relational ruptures and repair. And regardless of our primary vocational field or occupation, our age or relational status, those of us who study planetary cycles and symbols can verify for ourselves and attest to the world how we gain expanded understanding of ourselves and others and rise up to bravely meet every challenge and every evolutionary stage, guided by the sapphire ray of astrology's vastness, elegance, and exquisite tapestry.

Once again, I think anyone who resonates with this approach can adopt a therapeutic paradigm or frame and utilize astrology for emotional and psychological healing—not just professional therapists. But therapeutic astrology is an approach that's especially suitable for astrologers who get trained in counseling skills and learn about effective facilitation. Unlike the situation when I started out in this work, there are now a number of organizations that offer counseling skills training to astrologers, which is of immense benefit to the astrological field. It's also possible there are astrologers reading this who will consider whether pursuing some additional formal training might be a suitable path for your own life, to advance your career and increase your income potential, and in response to an inner call to service. And legally, in most countries you can't call yourself a therapist without the requisite license.

Practically speaking, to follow a career path merging astrology with a professional practice as a psychotherapist, one needs to earn some kind of credentials in the mental health field. Typically this involves completing a graduate degree in counseling psychology, clinical psychology, psychiatry, or social work, although the educational requirements vary in different countries. In the United States, graduate study is followed by internships and eventually passing a licensing examination. Realistically, it often takes several years to complete these tasks and enter the field as a fully credentialed professional. So whenever people ask me whether I think it's a good idea for them to pursue this arduous process, I usually respond that we should consider whether our own transits show an inclination to be a student for several years—for example, natal planets in Sagittarius, or in the 3rd or 9th houses, significant transits or progressions involving the 3rd or 9th houses, or involving natal or progressed Mercury or Jupiter; progressed aspects of Sun-Mercury or Sun-Jupiter; and progressed Mercury aspecting Jupiter, Saturn, Uranus, Neptune, and Pluto, all of which, in varying ways, show transformations of thought and advancing the progress of ideas. Transiting Saturn, the planet of work, discipline, and steady accomplishment, passing through the 3rd or 9th houses, aspecting planets in those houses, or aspecting natal Mercury also indicate that a concentrated period of education could be appropriate and desirable. I say all of this to affirm that embarking on this professional training requires a significant commitment. But I've found that the rewards of acquiring new emotional and interpersonal skills to accompany and support astrological knowledge have been well worth the effort.

I also want to acknowledge that some people don't want to carry the emotional weight of being a psychotherapist or a therapeutically oriented astrologer, and we should be honest with ourselves about that. In this kind of work, clients are going to tell you all kinds of things that are difficult to hear and to bear. The reality is that we're all going to feel the weight of Saturn somewhere in our work. If you work in accounting or financial services or computer systems or information science, you carry the weight of numbers and data. If you work in the real estate field it's the weight of information flow and showing up constantly for customer contacts. In academia, it's the weight of grading papers and preparing lecture notes and managing students in a classroom. But counseling can be a viable professional path if you have something in your chart that shows an interest in the psychotherapeutic process.

Moon represents emotions and the feeling function, therapy, self-care, and care of others. I find that psychotherapy as a career path is more fulfilling for people with natal Moon placed near an angle or making significant aspects to other planets (especially the Sun), or in the 10th house, or square the Midheaven, or the Moon is dispositor of the Cancer Midheaven, or aspects planets in the 10th house. This path is also congruent for those with natal planets in Cancer, or planets in the 4th house of feelings, clan, and ancestral influences. All of these can indicate emotional attunement and responsiveness, and an interest in family systems and family influences on mood and behavior. My natal Moon, ruler of my Cancer MC, is conjunct my Sun and aspects every planet in my chart. This is not to say that emotional development came easily to me; I've been undergoing therapy for decades. My mother had a Sun-Pluto conjunction and she had an undeniable force of character that greatly impacted me, so it has taken me a long time to straighten out my inner conditioning. I love therapy and never get enough of it, as I always find something I need to work through. And I'm convinced that the Moon—planet of moods, and symbol of constant change and renewal—is malleable and amenable to change in patterns. It can be refreshed and reorganized, and it can receive new imprints, so we actually start to feel better about our life.

Of course, many other planets play a role in furthering success in astrotherapy, including Mercury, which brings eloquence, zestful communication, and readiness for dialogue; Venus and the expression of affection, agreeableness, affability, and artistry in our work; Jupiter, which brings a wise, learned perspective to every human situation; and Saturn, lord of timing, strategy, and decision making. Uranus is important in astrotherapeutic work, as it imparts a sense of humor and an embrace of radical or immediate change. Neptune bestows intuition, a symbolic attitude, archetypal vision, imagination, serenity, surrender, trust in the universe, and a deepening immersion in meditation. Finally, Pluto is the symbol and agent of psychoanalytic investigation, the deep dive into our shadows, closure with the past, clearing of toxic resentments and fixations, and stages of renewal and empowerment.

I hope to have shown through this book's examples how astrology, united with psychotherapeutic practices and theories, can be a positive force for change in our human relationships, teaching us to love, accept, and cherish others more deeply, and to form more enduring and satisfying emotional attachments. Combined with psychological maps of human development and the evolution of personality, astrology can play an infinitely creative role in society, fostering the growth of centered, sane, and spiritually awakened individuals living harmoniously with others in an interdependent world.

Acknowledgments

For their friendship and abiding support I would like to express my warm thanks to Sid Aaronson, Claudia Bader, Lynn Bell, Agneta Borstein, Patricia Bowers, Ken Bowser, Margaret Cahill, Frank Clifford, Cathy Coleman, Armand Diaz, Ray Grasse, Dennis Harness, Tony Howard, Mark Jones, Brad Kochunas, Michael Lutin, Colleen Mauro, Shelley Montie, Bob Mulligan, Steve Pincus, David Railey, Kathy Rose, Jozef Slanda, Meire Santos, Richard and Victoria Smoot, Ena Stanley, Diana Syverud, Kay Taylor, Gisele Terry, Arlan Wise and Barbara Ybarra. I would especially like to thank the Organization for Professional Astrology (OPA), London School of Astrology, Astrology University, International Society for Astrological Research (ISAR), International Academy of Astrology, and NoDoor School of Astrology for the opportunity to present portions of the material in this book.

References

1. G. Bogart, *Dreamwork in Holistic Psychotherapy of Depression* (New York & London: Routledge, 2017); *Dreamwork and Self-Healing* (New York & London: Routledge, 2009); *Planets in Therapy: Predictive Technique and the Art of Counseling* (Lake Worth, FL: Ibis, 2012).

2. Z. Dobyns, *Expanding Astrology's Universe* (San Diego: ACS, 1983).

3. N. Tyl, *Holistic Astrology: The Analysis of Inner and Outer Environments* (Minneapolis: Llewellyn, 1980).

4. M. Mayer, *The Mystery of Personal Identity* (Berkeley, CA: BodyMindHealing Books, 2012).

5. A. Ruperti, *Cycles of Becoming* (Sebastopol, CA: CRCS, 1978), pp. 8–9.

6. J. Bugental, *Psychotherapy and Process* (New York: Random House, 1978), p. 60.

7. J. Bugental, *The Art of the Psychotherapist* (New York: Norton, 1987).

8. J. Bugental, *The Art of the Psychotherapist*, op cit., p. 40.

9. J. Gottman & N. Silver, *The Seven Principles for Making Marriage Work: A Practical Guide from the Country's Foremost Relationship Expert* (New York: Harmony, 1999).

About the Author

Greg Bogart, PhD is a licensed Marriage and Family Therapist who has also practiced astrology professionally since 1981. He is a lecturer in psychology at Sonoma State University, where he teaches courses on Jungian depth psychology, mythology, dreams, and the psychology of yoga. Previously he taught for 22 years in the Counseling Psychology, East–West Psychology, and Community Mental Health programs at California Institute of Integral Studies, John F. Kennedy University, Dominican University, and the Institute of Transpersonal Psychology. Greg is the author of *Astrology's Higher Octaves*; *Astrology and Spiritual Awakening*; *Planets in Therapy*: and *Astrology and Meditation: The Fearless Contemplation of Change*. His other books include *Dreamwork and Self-Healing*; *In the Company of Sages*; and *Dreamwork in Holistic Psychotherapy of Depression*.

Website: www.dawnmountain.com

email Greg at gbogart7@sbcglobal.net

Reviews for
Astrology & Meditation:
The Fearless Contemplation of Change

Greg Bogart's brilliant text is a ray of divine light that teaches us to use astrology with consciousness and intention for our highest spiritual evolution.

Dennis Harness, Ph.D., Academic Dean, Kepler College

In his new book Greg Bogart invites us to join him in a reverential and deeply felt contemplation of astrology. As the author puts it, 'If your life doesn't change, why study astrology?' It is not an exaggeration to say that this inspiring book from one of today's most respected astrology practitioners really can change your life.

Paul F. Newman, review in *The Astrological Journal* **(UK).**

This elegant book would be appealing and accessible to astrological novices looking for a spiritual approach to their interpretations. More advanced astrologers who are engaged in a meditative practice will be inspired by Greg Bogart's book as well. The book has many moving stories that demonstrate how the author guided his clients during stormy challenges in their lives.

Mary Plumb, review in *The Mountain Astrologer* **magazine**

In his inspiring new book, *Astrology and Meditation*, Greg Bogart explores the essential meanings of planets and signs with a strong spiritual perspective. Bogart views astrology as a form of active meditation, a spiritual practice that can lead to a deeper understanding of the evolution of one's soul. Bogart invites us to meditate on the spiritual lessons of the signs and planets. This may seem like elementary astrology but it is in fact essential astrology. Bogart explains the use of symbol amplification to enrich one's understanding of astrological symbols. Case histories throughout the book illuminate spiritual lessons that may be learned from various planetary pictures. The text ends with two must-read appendices: "Understanding the Jupiter-Saturn cycle" and "The Twelve Yogas of the Zodiac." Don't ignore the copious footnotes and the book's conclusion. There is a lot of valuable information to be found there.

Leda Blumberg, review in *Considerations* **magazine**

This is the *real* astrology. People who learn astrology should first learn this. Greg Bogart shows that people who study astrology need to have a spiritual practice, to meditate, to connect to their innate spirituality, and to a higher power. Only then can astrology help them, not otherwise.

Chakrapani Ullal, renowned Vedic Astrologer

If you want to know how astrological interpretation really works, if you desire to be able to read a chart in depth, then you must read this book, as it is one of the best books ever written about astrology. I have practiced astrology for many years, and don't read lots of books on it anymore. Most of them are written for beginners, or are sun sign books. Some are poorly written, or are extremely judgmental, or they repeat what others have already said. Yet a few books out there are jewels. There are the great teachings of Rudhyar, perhaps the greatest astrologer since Ptolemy. And there are others that I won't discuss here. Believe me, Astrology & Meditation deserves to be on that must-read list.

Greg Bogart is a philosopher, a psychotherapist, a psychologist, a university professor, a practitioner of many spiritual esoteric disciplines, including astrology. He pours all of his knowledge, acquired from years of study and practice, into this book. Moreover, he pours his heart into it too. That means that it's an experiential book: If you read and study its chapters, and really live in it as one must do with any profound book, then you will come to know more about astrology than ever before, and you will, if reading charts, see far deeper into any chart that you examine. You'll give better readings than you ever gave before.

If you are just beginning to study astrology, I recommend that you purchase this book, and read it. If I had discovered a book like Astrology & Meditation, when I was beginning my study of astrology, it would have saved me years of having to plough through bad books, faulty interpretations, and erroneous judgments. Even as an advanced astrologer, I find it a wonderful read. If you are employing astrology for healing, for growth, for counseling, or just studying it out of a general philosophical interest, you should get this book, read it, and absorb it. Then read it again, and keep it with you for the rest of your life.

Stuart Walker January 31, 2005 on www.amazon.com.

**Published by The Wessex Astrologer
and available from booksellers worldwide.
www.wessexastrologer.com**

www.ingramcontent.com/pod-product-compliance
Lightning Source LLC
Chambersburg PA
CBHW071222160426
43196CB00012B/2377